PLAYING THE GAME

Playing the Game: Lessons from a Life in Tennis

Copyright © 2024 by Bill Schillings

First paperback edition 2024

Editing by Kathy Brown
Book design by Kim Hall

ISBN 979-8-9903600-0-6 (paperback)
ISBN 979-8-9903600-1-3 (ebook)

www.billschillings.com

PRAISE FOR *PLAYING THE GAME*

"Weaving personal stories into the lessons learned from a life in tennis made for a powerful and inspirational message. I have the utmost respect for Bill as a coach and person. I could hear his voice coming off the pages."

—Peter Ayers (former ATP pro; All-American at Duke University; current coach of WTA player Emma Navarro)

"Bill Schillings has nailed it with *Playing the Game*. Somehow, he has put into words the steps needed to become a better tennis player, while keeping you smiling along the way with anecdotes from his personal experience. I watched him grow into an outstanding college player and now understand how he was able to make such significant strides. This is a 'can't miss' read for anyone who plays or coaches tennis. I couldn't put it down."

—Bob Bayliss (former men's tennis coach at Navy, MIT, and Notre Dame; fifth on all-time career wins list for Division 1 men's tennis; author of *Crosscourt Reflections*)

"Bill Schillings is a classic case of a person who *earned* success in the tennis world through preparation, perseverance, and competitive spirit. This book is a roadmap for players, parents, and coaches as they deal with the mental, physical, and emotional challenges of sports."

—Peter Daub (former men's tennis coach at William & Mary; three-time Colonial Athletic Association Coach of the Year)

"I remember meeting Bill at the Penn State tennis courts in the fall of his freshman year. He might have weighed 145 pounds soaking wet, but on the court his will to win and desire to improve was apparent from day one. I thoroughly enjoyed reading Bill's stories in *Playing the Game*. His 'lessons learned' on the court often transcend to 'life lessons' off the court. *Playing the Game* is just like Bill's tennis game: direct, hard-hitting, and straightforward."

—Tim McAvoy (former Penn State #1 player; seven-time platform tennis national champion; partner, Coho Partners)

"The lessons that unfold within *Playing the Game* are fantastic. I took notes because there's much I want to incorporate in my life, and much I want to share with others."

—Pender Murphy (former ATP player; three-time All-American at Clemson University; founder/director of TLA Tennis)

PLAYING THE GAME

LESSONS FROM A LIFE IN TENNIS

BILL SCHILLINGS

FOREWORD

I have spent my life around tennis, first as a player in high school and college and now as a high school coach. I love the sport, yet when people ask me about tennis, I find myself sharing stories—not about wins and losses, but about coaches who have demanded my best, doubles partners who became best friends, and my coming of age as I encountered my fiercest opponent, myself.

Today, I direct an organization called Silent Images, a nonprofit organization that provides professional video and photography at affordable prices for charities. I spend my professional life traveling the world with my camera chasing great stories. On a recent project, I sat down with Tom, who was a friend and hitting partner of tennis legend Arthur Ashe in the 1960s. As a white player growing up in Richmond, Virginia, this was not considered acceptable in the segregated society of that time and place. Nevertheless, Tom would sneak out at night to courts tucked away in the dark corners of the city to practice with Arthur. Through tennis, they shared a lifelong friendship that extended far beyond the sport and bridged the gap between white and black.

As Ashe was nearing his death, Tom visited him at his New York City apartment expecting to see all kinds of trophies lining his mantle. Yet, when he walked in, he was surprised to find Arthur sitting in a simple room with few adornments. Tom asked where the trophies were from his big wins at Wimbledon and the US Open. Ashe simply said, "Those are only a distraction to what is most important. It's my visitors who matter the most, Tom." At the end of his life, in sage-like fashion, Arthur Ashe had reminded Tom of what matters in life's journey. It's the people we meet and the imprint they make on our lives. It's not about reaching the final destination; it's about the relationships we build along the way, the lessons we learn that shape us into our best selves, and the stories that bring us together. Those always outshine any victory or loss in sports.

There are few people I've known in my life who exemplify this as well as Bill Schillings. I first met him as a thirteen-year-old kid when I rode my Huffy bike over to his tennis academy in Charlotte. My hope was to learn enough about the game to make my high school team. Since then, I've played under, coached alongside, and journeyed with Bill for many years. I found much more than a better forehand or volley during those years at his academy. I found a lifelong mentor and friend who helped shape my character and impacted my life well beyond the tennis court.

Playing the Game is a culmination of Bill's decades of experience in and around the sport of tennis. You'll find many useful principles and practices for becoming a better tennis player, but more importantly, this book will offer you lifelong lessons around topics like mentorship, generosity, humility, and learning to live a life of gratitude. You will find yourself smiling, laughing, and reflecting on your own story as Bill introduces us to the people he met along his journey and how they left him a better man. As it did for me, this book will inspire you to go and thank the people in your life who have impacted you in the same way.

—David Johnson
Founder and director, Silent Images; tennis coach,
Covenant Day School (Charlotte, NC)

CONTENTS

INTRODUCTION

This book is about my experiences playing the sport of tennis—how I started, where I finished, and who I met in between. It's about what I've learned and how that might apply to other people, whether it be in sports or any other pursuit in life. The main premise is that success requires going through five stages of development:

> **Ignition**—something, or someone, that initiates a passion within

> **Mentorship**—a relationship with an experienced and trusted advisor, trainer, or coach

> **Environment**—surroundings that foster conditions in which you thrive

> **Professionalism**—learning to conduct yourself with high standards

> **Humility**—accepting your limitations and embracing the opportunity to grow

The stages I experienced in tennis fell into these five categories—they represent my "path to success" (I use that term loosely since success is relative and has many definitions). For organizational purposes, I've arranged the stages chronologically, even though they overlapped and intertwined over a lifetime. Life can't be reduced to a formula, and our paths are often winding roads rather than superhighways.

Much of what follows will appeal to those interested in improving their tennis game, but if you're looking for a comprehensive textbook, this book will probably disappoint. Sometimes, too much detail can get in the way. I think that has some truth in any field of endeavor—sports, business, spirituality, fitness, nutrition, and so on. This book views things from 30,000 feet rather than ground level. Because if you get the big picture right, the details tend to take care of themselves.

So . . . I suppose it's best to start with a little about my road in tennis. The short version is that I had some moderate success in my playing days. I became the best player in the small pond of fish with whom I swam in high school and college. Then I tried my hand at pro tennis—a much bigger pond, lots of big fish. I shared the court with some of my generation's best players. And I had the good fortune to learn a lot about tennis and life from some great coaches.

After spending many years playing competitive tennis, I've spent the bulk of my adult life coaching the sport. One lesson I learned as a coach was that if I wanted a message to be received *and* retained by my students, then it was usually best to accompany it with a story. So, this book is part memoir, part manual—it contains stories about my experiences and the lessons I learned from them. One of my favorite authors, Steven Pressfield, recently wrote a blog post about his own book, *Govt Cheese: A Memoir,* saying, "The beats of my story might not match those of yours, but they will sure parallel them metaphorically." We glean value from listening to other people's stories because we can learn lessons that apply to our journeys from those walking a similar path. The five stages I've listed here apply to anyone's journey, although each person's story will surely be different than mine.

Naturally, stories rely on the teller's memory. But, as John Steinbeck points out in his book *Travels with Charley,* "The memory is at best a faulty, warpy reservoir . . . the whole bundle wracked until objectiveness is nigh impossible." The stories in this book are not intended to reflect history in the truest sense of the word. They reflect how I've remembered events based on my perception, personality, and patterns of thought.

In *The Things They Carried,* Tim O'Brien writes, "The thing about remembering is that you don't forget. You take your material where you find it, which is in your life, at the intersection of past and present. The memory-traffic feeds into a rotary up on your head, where it goes in circles for a while, then pretty soon imagination flows in and the traffic merges and shoots off down a thousand different streets. As a writer, all you can do is pick a street and go for the ride, putting things down as they come at you . . . story-truth is truer sometimes than happening-truth."

These quotes sum up, better than I ever could, my thoughts as I wrote this book. I know my memory is "a faulty, warpy reservoir." But I've taken solace in the idea that "story-truth is truer sometimes than happening-truth"—I think lessons can be found in both. The stories are simply a conduit through which the messages are transmitted. I have no illusions that my successes or failures in tennis hold any value beyond that. My hope is that they will reflect something that's true and applicable in your own experience.

PART 1
LESSONS

CHAPTER 1
IGNITION

I've always been intrigued by how successful people get their start—what initiates the passion in them that leads to a lifetime pursuit of excellence. In *The Talent Code*, Daniel Coyle calls this starting point "ignition." He describes it as "a hot, mysterious burst, an awakening . . . the set of signals and subconscious forces that create our identity; the moments that lead us to say *that is who I want to be* . . . it burns just out of our awareness, largely within our unconscious mind."

I started thinking about ignition watching my high school chemistry teacher, Mr. Oberkrieser (yes, that was his real name). I'd never seen anyone as knowledgeable or passionate about any one subject. I wondered when he first fell in love with chemistry and where passion like his came from. Even though I didn't care about chemistry, his enthusiasm was infectious, and I loved to listen to his stories. One of his favorites was about how much he enjoyed spending long hours with his buddies in the chemistry lab during college. At the time, my conception of college included zero hours spent in a chemistry lab. But even then, I found myself hoping that one day I would be as passionate about something as Mr. O was about chemistry.

Here are a few things I asked myself as my mind wandered in the back of his classroom (hoping he wouldn't call on me to answer any questions): When did he know he wanted to become a chemist? How did he come to know so much about chemistry? Were there other people who knew and cared as much about chemistry as he did? (I found that hard to fathom.) How did he develop such passion? Didn't he ever get tired of teaching kids like me? Why wasn't he famous or rich?

Some of the answers came to me many years later when I realized that, incredibly, I had become just like Mr. Oberkrieser. I was teaching a junior tennis clinic and giving an impassioned talk about how awesome the sport of tennis was. I was deep in the weeds telling stories about my college days playing tennis and illustrating arcane points about tactics, technique, and sports psychology. I have no idea what made me think of Mr. O—maybe it was the blank stares from the kids. The topic was different, but the dynamics were identical. Tennis had become as much a part of my DNA as chemistry was to his. I probably seemed like an expert to the kids, although one they could hardly understand. I was certain some were silently asking the same questions I had asked about Mr. O, but that was okay. I knew I'd have an impact, even if none of those kids became pro tennis players or coaches. Heck, I still remembered Mr. O's class forty years later because I learned things about calling, passion, enthusiasm, and dedication that went far beyond the fine points of chemical reactions.

So, what are the ignition moments that lead to becoming like Mr. O in a chemistry class, or me teaching a tennis clinic? I don't know what they were for Mr. O but, ironically, around the same time I was taking his class, I was in the midst of ignition in a much different endeavor. As you may have figured out, it took place on a tennis court rather than in a chemistry lab.

Liftoff

One spring weekend when I was eleven, I watched my first tennis match on TV. It was between Rod Laver and Ken Rosewall—yes, this makes me feel ancient. Since we are now in the age of Google, I did a search and found the highlights.[1] Apparently, this was quite a historic match; it's been called the "match that made tennis in the United States."[2] It certainly had a lifelong impact on me.

Laver and Rosewall made tennis look easy and fun, so I was inspired to give it a try. I hunted down an old tennis racket

---

1 https://youtu.be/SuNWnzNsVmw
2 https://www.tennis.com/news/articles/1972-the-rod-laver-vs-ken-rosewall-wct-final-in-dallas

in the garage, hopped on my bike, and headed down to the tennis courts near our house to hit against the backboard. I tried to emulate their strokes and soon realized things weren't as easy as the pros made it look. I spent most of my time chasing down the balls I hit over the backboard. Even though I could only manage a rally of two to three shots, something happened in my psyche that I can't explain: I knew I was meant to be a tennis player. To this day, my tennis game is based on what I saw on a spring afternoon in 1972 . . . and I've gotten pretty good at hitting on a backboard.

Never underestimate the power of ignition—just one moment can have a lifelong impact.

Parent Power

My dad noticed my newfound interest in tennis, so he offered to play with me before going to work. Most mornings that summer, we headed down to the courts and played sets. He offered no formal instruction; I don't think he had very much experience (if any) with the technical side of the sport. That didn't bother us; we just wanted to play the game. But somehow, even though he was also essentially a beginner at tennis, he destroyed me every time. Being an engineer, he enjoyed keeping statistics—a piece of paper appeared taped to his bedroom door. One column had "Kid" at the top followed by zeroes and ones. The other had "Pop" followed by endless sixes. He seemed to take perverse pleasure in this, so naturally, I was motivated to get revenge. Maybe my dad knew that his record-keeping would "ignite" my interest in ways nothing else could. Who knows? Either way, when he went off to work, I played tennis most of the day and started to improve. By the following summer, his victories became more infrequent, and that piece of paper on his closet door disappeared. But he had fanned my spark of interest in tennis, which is all I think he cared about anyway.

As my interest in the sport grew, so did my dad's. As my unofficial coach, he had more criticism than praise, although I sensed that as a father, he was my biggest fan. This could be confusing at times. Occasionally I'd be at his office, and it surprised me to hear one of his coworkers say, "Oh, you're the tennis player your dad has told us so much about." Or we would be watching tennis on TV and, after an amazing shot by John McEnroe, my dad would turn to me and say, "You could hit that shot just as well."

Years later, when I was in my late twenties, I won a doubles exhibition tournament with Jim Courier (at that time a teenager ranked top thirty in the world). That evening, I heard Pop say to my wife, "Bill carried the team." To me, comments like those were disconnected from reality. True, I could occasionally hit a shot like McEnroe, and, yes, I had held my own playing with Courier. But I hadn't achieved anywhere near what those players had. I couldn't figure out whether to take his comments as encouragement or feel bad that I hadn't lived up to his expectations. I think these are examples of the dilemma any parent has when commenting on their kids' pursuits. Well-intentioned comments can be misinterpreted and constructive feedback taken the wrong way. I'll leave that discussion for another time and place.[3] In the end, I know that without my dad's interest and support, I never would have become ignited to play tennis or achieved what I did in later years.

My dad didn't see me play much in high school. We had just moved to Buffalo, New York, where he worked long hours as the project manager for the construction of a steel mill. No doubt he had more important things to do. But that was just as well. Whenever he was around, I tensed up and played poorly. I don't know if this was due to an inordinate desire to impress him or that I felt he'd be evaluating my every move. Likely some of both.

When I was a freshman in college, he came to watch a match that I won 6-0, 6-1. The only game my opponent won came on my serve after a few mindless double faults. After the match, my dad brought those double faults to my attention and pointed out that I needed to be more disciplined mentally. Of course, there was some truth to that, but I think he realized at this point that he may have been contributing to the problem. He rarely appeared at my matches during my

---

3 I wrote a book on this topic called *Sports Parenting: Creating an Environment for Success . . . without Going Bat Sh*t Crazy.*

college career . . . until late in my senior year when we were playing one of the better teams in the country. By that time, I had matured and was well established as a college player. At the match he attended, I was still slightly distracted, but thankfully, my dad had disconnected from his role as evaluator of my tennis game. I didn't get the sense that he was taking mental notes to render a critique after the match. He seemed proud of what I had achieved in college tennis and content to simply enjoy the moment. This enabled me to focus on what I was doing and play well. I still remember that match as one of my favorites in college, even though I lost, mainly because I shared it with my dad.

> *Parents often have an important role in ignition. They can be your harshest critics but biggest fans. Accept and embrace the dichotomy—the trade-off is worth it.*

Rabbits and Role Models

One night during my first summer playing tennis, I was bored and took a ride on my bike down to the courts. The lights were on, which I found interesting since I didn't know you could play tennis at night. Just two players were out there—one a serious-looking adult, the other a kid my age looking just as intense. They weren't competing, just rallying with flawless control and consistency. Except for the pop of the ball hitting a racket, it was dead quiet. I was transfixed. It felt like I had stumbled upon a church service, the kind that I'd want to attend every day. Their strokes looked like Laver and Rosewall on TV, and everything they did seemed effortless as they hit patterns of shots—forehands crosscourt, backhand to forehand down the line, and so on. This blew my mind. I had no idea kids my age could hit a tennis ball that well.

Both players were dressed impeccably in matching tennis outfits; they even had little tennis towels folded into their shorts to wipe the beads of sweat from their foreheads. I had neither seen clothes specifically made for tennis players nor towels that small. I found out later that the older guy was a tennis pro, which made sense. The kid my age was his student who was preparing to play tournaments against other kids who were just as good as he was. I had no idea how that might be possible, but I did know one thing: I *needed* to learn to play tennis like that. Thankfully, I can report that I've long since achieved that goal. However, I've never taken for granted my ability to hit a tennis ball with some proficiency, as I always remember sitting on my bike watching those guys hit . . . wondering if I'd ever get that good.

That kid's name was Bill Beneke. He lived in my neighborhood, and we became friends playing tennis for one of the best high school teams in the area. He beat me badly the first few times we played, but in our last two years of high school I became slightly stronger. I have a theory on how that happened.

Tennis players fall along a continuum based on their backgrounds and temperaments. At one end are "players" who focus more on outcome. On the other end are "hitters" who focus more on technique. Due to his early exposure to tennis pros, proper mechanics, and so on, I think Bill was more of a hitter. I played several other sports growing up, so I was more of a player. As a result, Bill was slightly better than me technically, but I had an edge when it came to athleticism and competitiveness. Also, Bill was an "A" student who wanted to become a doctor (which he did). He had more perspective on sports, and life, than I did. Maybe winning a tennis match wasn't the only thing that mattered to him. I, on the other hand, had little to no perspective nor vision in life beyond winning and losing tennis matches. This may have had its advantages on the tennis court, but it's debatable whether this mindset was a net positive in the big picture. I will say that win or lose, Bill always handled himself with sportsmanship, integrity, and character beyond his years. To this day, when I hear someone use the expression "class act," I immediately think of Bill Beneke.

My wife, Liz, was an academic high-achiever and valedictorian of her high school class. She once shared with me that what motivated her most in high school was one of her classmates, George Irwin, whom she considered the smartest kid in her class. Liz referred to George as her "rabbit"—meaning the person she was going to chase down and overtake through hard work, determination, and competitive spirit. Yet again, this description made me think of Bill Beneke. Liz needed George just as I needed Bill; they were the rabbits that ignited us. I don't think either one of us would have achieved what we did without them.

> *Ignition happens when you find your rabbit*
> *and start chasing it.*

Visualization

By my junior year in high school, I had become one of the better players in western New York (I went to Orchard Park High School, in a suburb of Buffalo). That year, 1977, I qualified to compete in the regional tournament that determined who would go to the state championships. The dominant player that year was a twelve-year-old named Jimmy Arias (yes, you read that right—he was twelve). As junior tennis legends go, you can't get bigger than Jimmy Arias. He was the best junior in the area, could beat all the adults, and was possibly the best player his age in the world. I was excited to see him play. When I got off the bus at the regional tournament, I made a beeline to the court where Jimmy was dismantling a kid twice his size. He wasn't hard to find—I just followed the hum of the crowd until I found him. I had pictured a big, strong kid, but Jimmy wasn't very big. Rather, *scrawny* would be the word that comes to mind. But the kid was an insane tennis player. He had it all:

consistency, control, and pace. When his racket met the ball, it was moving lightning fast. I'm still not sure where all that power came from. If I had tried to swing that hard, I'm certain I would have missed eight out of ten times.

Jimmy moved like a cheetah chasing an antelope—agile, powerful, and deadly. When he had maneuvered his opponent out of position, he calmly hit a winner to the open court. He did all this without tensing up or over-hitting. For a kid that age, he was unusually composed and confident. I envied him—all these qualities were ones I had yet to develop. But what stuck with me most was the trajectory of Jimmy's shots (tennis pros call this "shape"). When his ball cleared the net, it was so high that I thought it was going out every time. Somehow, just at the last moment, the topspin he generated with that massive racket speed made the ball drop just inside the baseline. I'd never seen anyone hit with such depth and consistency. That visual has stayed with me to this day.

I would like to say Jimmy was a rabbit for me. But I couldn't conceive of how I could get close enough to catch him. He won the regionals easily, so the three guys who qualified for the states were, in order: Jimmy Arias, Peter DeBraun (a tall, muscular senior), and me. We traveled together to the state tournament, so I got to know Jimmy a little bit. He was humble, personable, mature above his years, and handled the pressure of being a tennis celebrity well. Soon after, he ended up in Florida at one of the first full-time tennis academies catering to aspiring pros.

He turned pro at sixteen and made it to number five in the world by the time he was nineteen.[4] It's been a long time since my high school days, but for years I've been trying to hit my groundstrokes with the same "shape" as Jimmy's . . . it's still a work in progress. Ignition like that never wears off.

> *Ignition is unpredictable. We never know when, or how, it will happen. But most of the time some inspiring person will be involved—it could even be a twelve-year-old kid.*

---

4 https://www.youtube.com/watch?v=iFDGfhFZWVk)

CHAPTER 2
MENTORSHIP

I f you want to become successful, it's helpful to find a good coach. If you're fortunate, you might also find a mentor for a lifetime, which is a much bigger deal. My high school tennis coach, Terry McMahon, fell into the latter category. The relatively short period when he coached me in tennis was the conduit through which mentorship bloomed. Not everyone is blessed with great mentors. Author Jim Collins calls this "who" luck, "when you come across somebody who changes your trajectory or invests in you, bets on you, gives you guidance and key points."[5] Time and chance certainly play a part, but there's also an element of volition on the part of the recipient. "Luck

5 The Knowledge Project podcast, Ep. #67, Oct. 1, 2019

is what happens when preparation meets opportunity"[6]—meaning we can't control when or where the opportunity will present itself, but we can be prepared when it does. So, when a mentor appears, it's up to you to seize the opportunity. That takes awareness, receptivity, and humility.

The first time Terry McMahon registered on my radar was when I went out for the tennis team my sophomore year. His presence demanded respect, so we all called him Mr. McMahon. It would be many years until I could even think of calling him Terry. I suspect most of his former students/players feel the same way. With those closest to him, he's most comfortable simply being addressed as "T," which seems appropriate and just like him—solid, simple, gets the job done. During my teen years, Mr. McMahon was in his mid-thirties, and he cut an imposing figure to us twerpy teenagers. A former football player and coach, he was built like a small truck, had red hair and a crew cut (true to his Irish Catholic roots), and was an amazing tennis player. I would describe his demeanor as no-nonsense. He demanded your respect and required you to earn his, both on the court and off. If you were on Mr. McMahon's bad side, I doubt you'd ever find a tougher adversary; if you were on his good side, you'd never find a better advocate. Thankfully, I found myself on the right side of that equation. Our relationship has lasted now for close to fifty years. I can't think of

---

6 A quote attributed to the philosopher Seneca, a long time ago

anyone I respect more. And I know I've earned his respect as well. This is a good feeling.

I was lucky my path crossed Terry McMahon's during my formative years. What follows are a few anecdotes from a lifetime of experiences with him. They illustrate qualities to look for in finding a mentor for your own journey through life. If you can find someone with just a few of these attributes, you will have done well. If you find someone with all of them, consider yourself very fortunate indeed. And for goodness' sake, keep in mind that the best way to return the favor is to look for the opportunity to mentor someone else.

Credibility

When I went out for his team as a neophyte fifteen-year-old, it didn't take long for Mr. McMahon to establish credibility with me. He had an armload of Wilson T-2000 tennis rackets that were just like the ones used by Jimmy Connors, the world's number one player at the time. He could hit the ball incredibly hard, easily beat any of us kids, and played tournaments on weekends. When he won a tournament, which was often, he always provided the same cryptic response about the results: "It went well." All this made a big impression on me. Maybe it was because I only had one tennis racket and couldn't hit the ball very hard. Or that I had yet to play in a tournament, let alone win one—if I had, I would have wanted everyone to know.

Considering all this, it should come as no surprise that if Mr. McMahon said, *Jump*, I said, *How high?* And as you might expect, I absorbed everything he told me about tennis. To this day, I remember many of his coaching tips—reach for the ceiling to hit a topspin serve; don't crush every overhead; when you play in front of a crowd, keep your eyes on the court. Whatever the advice, I'd find myself thinking, *Well, that worked really well; why didn't I think of it?* Years later, I shared those same tips with my own students, which is just one example of how Mr. McMahon's impact extended far beyond the time and place in which we first met.

> *Mentorship begins with establishing credibility, both in form and substance.*

Commitment

Our high school was in the "snow belt" just south of Buffalo, where the long winters were not exactly conducive to developing your tennis game. We practiced on Friday nights at the indoor tennis center when no one else wanted to play. We finished around 10 p.m. and by that time, it was cold and dark outside. Quite often, the sweat on my hair froze as I walked from the front door to the car after practice. When spring finally came, we often had to clear snow off the courts to play outside. I mention these anecdotes not to elicit sympathy but to point out something I didn't consider until years later. Even though Mr. McMahon had a full-time job and a wife and kids, he was always the first to arrive and the last to leave. I'm sure he was just as cold as we were getting to his car after practice and didn't love shoveling snow off tennis courts either, but his commitment never wavered. That example has stayed buried in my psyche my whole life. So, when I found myself in the role of coach years later, I tried to exhibit the same commitment I'd seen in Mr. McMahon. By the way, Orchard Park has been the perennial best high school tennis team in western New York since I played there in the 1970s, and Terry McMahon continues to coach the team as I write this in 2024—now that's commitment.

Mentors lead from the front and teach by example.

Presence

Among the players I competed against in western New York, the best was John Termotto. He had a national ranking, which sounded impressive, even though I was clueless about how to attain one. He won all the tournaments I played in and, according to rumors, had beaten Jimmy Arias (the child prodigy superstar mentioned in the last chapter). The first time I played John, he beat me so badly I can't remember if I even got one game. The second time I fared slightly better, although I still lost badly. When he shook my hand at the end, he commented that my "groundies" were improving. However, he said this in a way that I found dismissive and condescending. It was clear, at least to my highly sensitive and competitive mind, that John didn't consider me to be any threat on the tennis court. This really burned my biscuit. I couldn't wait to play him again. The next two matches we played were the most memorable of my junior tennis career—mainly because of what I learned about mentorship from Mr. McMahon.

The first match was at an indoor court during a tournament for players sixteen and under. As usual, John was the top seed. Since this was a United States Tennis Association (USTA) sanctioned tournament, rather than a high school match, my mom took me to the event. I was so eager to play that when our names were called, I raced to the scorer's table to get the balls and headed out to the court. I wasn't inclined to walk out with John and make small talk. When I got there, I went to open the new balls, which come in pressurized cans with rings on top. You put your index finger in the ring and pull back the metal lid. As I did this, my fingers just happened to be in the wrong place. The razor-sharp edge of the lid sliced into the middle finger of my right hand (I play right-handed), creating a little flap of skin. It didn't hurt much, but during warm-up, it started to bleed. I tried to act natural even as tiny drops of blood started to fall on the court. To put it mildly, I was concerned. I had never anticipated anything like this and didn't need the distraction in what, to me, was the most important match of my young tennis career. I did what any self-respecting teenager in this emotional state would do: I looked over to my mom, hoping she could somehow fix the problem. When I did, I was shocked to see Mr. McMahon standing right next to her. I had no idea he knew I was playing in the tournament, let alone cared enough to attend on a Saturday afternoon. I did the best I could and prayed the tournament officials didn't notice my blood droplets on their court.

About ten minutes later, Mr. McMahon appeared at the back of the court. He had jumped in this car, somehow found the closest drugstore (this was in the days before GPS apps), bought Band-Aids, antibiotic ointment, and tape, then raced back to the tennis center. He delivered them to me between games. I wrapped my finger and played okay; all things considered. But the result was the same: I found myself, once again, receiving that condescending handshake after the match . . . as I tried not to get too much blood on John.

I share this not because that match means much in the scheme of things. The fact that Mr. McMahon showed up meant everything, and I've never forgotten it. His presence validated me as a tennis player at a time when I needed it most. Certain people have the potential to do that more than others. In that moment, and during those next few years, no one was more affirming to me than Mr. McMahon. And all it took was for him to show up, to simply be *present*, at a tennis match.

The next match I played against John was during the spring of my senior year. I knew it would be the last time our paths crossed because my family was moving out of the state. I had qualified as the best player in my region to go to the state high school championship (Jimmy Arias had left to go to Florida by this time). I won my first match and, sure enough, who was next up on the draw sheet? John Termotto. This would, without question, be the biggest match of my junior tennis career. Thankfully, this being a high school event, I knew that Mr. McMahon's presence was a foregone conclusion. I'll spare you the details of the match other than to say I didn't cut myself on the can of balls, it took a few hours to play, and when the third set tiebreaker ended, I was the player moving on to the next round. After shaking hands with John—who, to his credit, was quite respectful and sportsmanlike—I looked over to Mr. McMahon. I'll never forget the look of pride on his face . . . he didn't have to say a thing.

Mentors show up—they're around when you need them most.

Connections

I spent many hours hanging around the indoor tennis club where Mr. McMahon taught tennis. As one of his protégés, I often found myself in the company of his tennis community.

One of my favorites was a guy named Desi Tamasy. To my teenage brain, Desi was ancient (probably around the same age I am as I write this). He was one of those guys you sometimes run across in the tennis world who seem as if they live at the club and sleep in the back room on a cot. Mr. McMahon set me up to play sets with Desi one day. Here's what I knew about Desi at the time: he was a friend of Mr. McMahon's (most important), he looked old, he played a lot of tennis tournaments, and he had a heavy Hungarian accent that made him hard to understand.

As we warmed up, I remember thinking, *This guy doesn't hit the ball very hard, doesn't move very well, and doesn't seem to be paying much attention. How hard can this be?* He then proceeded to run my cocky teenage butt all over the court. And he rarely, if ever, made an error. In about thirty minutes, Desi had beaten me easily and we were at the net shaking hands. Then he gave me some advice that I've never forgotten, and I've passed it along to countless students many times as a coach. He said, in his heavy accent, "Beel, you don't have to heet it so much for the line!" I had just gotten good enough to hit the ball hard and close to the lines—although, admittedly, I wasn't very consistent. Apparently, in my enthusiasm to win the set against this "old guy," I may have been a tad overaggressive. Occasionally, I would hit a winner,[7] which was all I

---

7 A winner, in tennis terms, is when you hit a ball that bounces twice before your opponent gets to it. They are fun to hit but high risk and often result in errors. In my teenage boy mind, winners were associated with hitting hard, spectacular shots low over the net and close to the lines. Playing with that mentality is like playing baseball and trying to hit a home run every time.

cared about. At the time, I considered this synonymous with tennis ability. I didn't notice I was getting beaten badly, or how exhausted I was, until it was over.

Of course, I now know that there's an inverse relationship between power and control. Desi was insane at control and knew that my propensity to hit hard, particularly so close to the lines, would mean that I'd miss too much and be very easy to beat. I needed to play with more margin for error, a topic about which I was clueless. Hence, his advice to not "heet so much for the line." Desi was the Yoda to my Luke Skywalker. I may have had some potential, but I didn't know how to put it to use. To put it bluntly, I played like an idiot. To put it tactfully, I had a limited understanding of how important discipline, tactics, or mental skills were to success on a tennis court. Desi summed this all up in one sentence. He was the perfect role model for how to play the sport—and I'm certain that was why Mr. McMahon orchestrated our connection.

Many years later, I asked Mr. McMahon whatever happened to Desi Tamasy. He said Desi had passed away suddenly from a massive heart attack during a tennis tournament. I knew there was some sadness there for Mr. McMahon, as Desi was well-respected and a great friend. But he said it was the most fitting way for Desi to pass, still playing tennis until his last day, enjoying the sport that he loved. Desi's legacy lives on in my mind and spirit. And I've never forgotten the lessons I learned from him on the tennis court.

Mentors know how to connect you with the right people at the right times.

Wisdom

It's hard to believe that after I graduated high school, I didn't cross paths with Mr. McMahon again until nearly twenty years later. I was teaching a ladies' clinic at my tennis club in Charlotte, North Carolina, and noticed a car drive past and park. I saw someone get out and walk toward the courts, not recognizing who it was until I heard his unmistakable, New York-accented voice say, "Hey, you know where I might find Willie Schillings?" I knew it was Mr. McMahon since he alone called me that, but it didn't matter—I would have known his voice anywhere. Apparently, he was playing a tournament in Atlanta, knew I lived in Charlotte, and figured he'd just stop by for a visit—mind you, Atlanta is a good four-hour drive from Charlotte. (We all need more people in our lives who can show up unannounced and know they are welcome; Mr. McMahon is one of those people to me.) I introduced him to the ladies, finished the clinic, and called my wife to see if we might have room for a houseguest that evening.

By this time, I was well into my own career as a coach. That evening, after we caught up, I sought his advice on some coaching issues I'd been struggling with. One was that I tended to be overly self-critical. No matter how well a lesson or clinic had gone, I always felt I could have done something better. I hoped that at some point my critical inner voice would quiet down, and I could coast a bit—or, in other words, not have to try so hard. I was looking for confirmation from Mr. McMahon in this regard. To the contrary, he shared that he'd been dealing with that same voice for years. And he didn't ever expect that battle to end. He wasn't looking to coast; he was still looking for ways to get better. This helped me understand that coaching, like playing, is a never-ending process of self-improvement—some degree of self-critique and effort is essential to do it well.

I also asked for his thoughts regarding a young lady I was coaching. She had recently lost her dad due to a massive heart attack. Her father had spent countless hours with her on the court, and she had asked if I could give her more lessons in hopes of filling this gap. While I was committed to doing whatever I could to help, I was hesitant because I felt that offering more lesson time wouldn't be the best use of her mom's money. I thought it might be better for her to attend more clinics and practice with a wider range of players.

Mr. McMahon disagreed. He said if the girl was a hard worker, which she was, and would make the most of the extra time, which she would, then I shouldn't resist. I flashed back to when I was sixteen and my dad had a heart attack (fortunately, he survived). Mr. McMahon was one of the few people who knew of our family's struggles at the time, and he went out of his way to help. Now I had the opportunity to pay it forward. I called the next day to schedule those extra lessons. Once again, Mr. McMahon had shown up at just the right time. His advice may have been contrary to my instincts, but, considering the source, I didn't have much choice but to embrace it.

Addendum to this story: that visit wasn't purely a gabfest on coaching. At my house that evening, I introduced him with great pleasure to my wife and two daughters (then ten and eight). My kids were mesmerized by this energetic, fast-talking guy who used to coach their dad. He was like a lovable, kick-ass grandfather who appeared at our dinner table out of nowhere. The highlight of the evening was watching him play Ringolevio with the girls. What's that? Well . . . this is a game Mr. McMahon had learned during his New York City upbringing, though neither I nor anyone in my family had heard of it. I suggest you look up the rules on Google. For now, let's just say it's an intense version of tag involving running, yelling, and general mayhem. Although it's probably best played outside, Mr. McMahon set this game up in the house. I doubt my wife would have stood for this if it had been my idea. I hadn't seen my kids (or our dog) have that much fun in quite some time. To this day, when I mention my former coaches, the first thing they ask is, "Is that the Ringolevio guy?" They are in their thirties now, and I guarantee they would play this game tomorrow if I could explain the rules like Mr. McMahon.

Mentors say what you need to hear, not what you want to hear.

Generosity

About twenty more years passed. Mr. McMahon and his wife, Diane, were visiting some family in North Carolina and needed a place to stay for a few nights. By that time, he was in his eighties and moving slower, but incredibly, Mr. McMahon was still coaching the high school team in Orchard Park. Despite his age, his energy level was undiminished, and his mind was sharp as ever. I had to concentrate to keep up.

He tagged along one afternoon to observe as I taught lessons. Emma, a teenage player I was working with, was preparing to try out for her high school team. My former coach took a special interest and struck up a conversation with her. She was a hard worker with a great attitude, and he had picked up on how eager she was to learn. His radar for such things was unchanged from when he had taken interest in me as a teenager. Emma had some time after our lesson, so I suggested they go to an adjacent court and work on her serve. I eavesdropped as I taught another student. Mr. McMahon was truly in his element. At first Emma didn't know what to make of this eighty-year-old bundle of energy. But as he offered tips on her game, it was obvious that he knew what he was talking about. I could tell she was all in.

He observed that she was too comfortable hitting down the middle of the court and needed to play more aggressively by hitting closer to the sidelines (the opposite of how I played at her age). Typical of his football-influenced coaching style, where you assign names to plays, he called the former tactic "kumquat" and the latter "bingo." I can guarantee that Emma will always remember "kumquat" and "bingo," and I'm certain it was the best thing she learned about tennis that day. Within just a few minutes, Mr. McMahon had built an impactful relationship with Emma. As her coach, I'd had nothing to do with this, other than being the guy who connected her with Mr. McMahon. He had done the same for me many years before when he connected me with Desi Tamasy . . . I had a deeper understanding of the term "circle of life" by the end of that day.

Mentors are always looking to share their passion and expertise with anyone willing to learn.

CHAPTER 3
ENVIRONMENT

By the end of my senior year in high school, I was one of the top tennis players in the state of New York and aspired to play in college. My parents took me on visits to some smaller schools, and a few of them offered me athletic scholarships. But once I stepped onto the campus of Penn State University, I knew that was where I wanted to go. The problem was that Penn State's coach only recruited nationally ranked players. He was nice enough, however, to meet with us and offered to help get me accepted to the school. He explained that I'd be a "walk-on," which meant that I'd be allowed to try out, but he would not be offering any scholarship money unless I made the top three on the team. It was clear he thought that was a remote possibility.

Challenge

When I first walked through the doors at the indoor tennis center at Penn State, I was an insecure, skinny, seventeen-year-old freshman. Two guys on court one were hitting tennis balls harder than I had ever seen. I assumed they were former Penn State players now on the pro tour. My heart sank when I learned they were on the team. One was named Alex Davidson, he was the only senior that year. He was built like a football player and carried himself with a quiet confidence that I envied. He was practicing with a junior, Bill Schmucker, whose association with Alex gave him immediate credibility in my eyes. Both were bigger, stronger, and, in my mind, better than me. I felt like a boy walking among men, certain I had made a big mistake choosing Penn State.

Over the next week, our coach, Holmes Cathrall, had all the players compete to determine positions on the team. These "challenge matches" were highly competitive, intense affairs. You could argue that pitting teammates against each other might not be the best way to build camaraderie. Of course, that was not my decision to make. I could only assume that Coach Cathrall, a former Marine Corps captain, figured that quickly weeding out the weak links on the team took precedence over protecting my fragile freshman psyche.

Therefore, it came as no surprise that Alex and Bill were among the first players Coach Cathrall had me play against. This led to the first of many lessons I was to learn through college tennis: never pre-judge outcomes based on appearances. Once I got on the other side of the net, my perspective changed. First, the ball seemed to move slower, which meant I had more time to react than I had thought. Second, I realized people miss more often in competition than when hitting cooperatively in practice. And last, I understood how emotions played a big part. Once we started to compete, I sensed that Alex and Bill were just as nervous as I was. All these factors were to my benefit, and I ended up winning both matches and playing number three on the team that season.

Competing well in those matches was a crucial step in my development. It taught me a great deal about psychological dynamics and provided a glimmer of hope that I could be successful at the college level. Without that confidence boost, I never would have become the player I was four years later. Maybe Coach Cathrall knew what he was doing after all.

Embrace environments that push you beyond your comfort zone. Perception doesn't always reflect reality— quite often, you're better than you think.

Vision

The other player that stood out to me during that first year was Tim McAvoy. He was a junior and our number one player—lightning-fast, aggressive, and competitive. There was no disconnect between my perception and reality; I truly was nowhere close to his level. However, for an impressionable freshman like me, Tim was the perfect role model.

In one of my first team matches, we played one of our rivals, Temple University. I lost my singles match quickly due to a combination of inexperience, nerves, and a much stronger opponent. My attention immediately turned to watching Tim play Temple's top player, Omar Sebastian. I had never seen, in person, tennis played at that level before. They were both not only good tennis players but great athletes, and their power, consistency, and intensity were well beyond any of the players on either team.

Somewhere late in the match, Tim hit what looked to me like a winner. However, he saw the ball out. Omar was on the sideline furthest from where the ball had landed and had called it in. Tim motioned Omar up to the net and told him that the ball had been out—in effect, he took the point from himself. I was stunned. I couldn't imagine doing this myself. The rules in tennis are that you call the balls on your side of the net. Since Omar had called the ball in, Tim had every right to take the point. As I watched their brief discussion, it was clear that, even though they were fierce competitors, they had developed a mutual respect. Omar accepted Tim's judgment, took the point, and then they resumed the match. I've never forgotten that lesson in sportsmanship; it was one of many I would learn from Tim over the next two years.

After the match, Tim found me sitting alone, upset about losing and letting the team down. He explained that the player I had lost to, a senior, had compiled the best record in Temple's history over the previous three seasons. He said I needed to put the match in perspective, let it go, and get ready to play doubles, which was where many college matches were won and lost. In later years, I remembered that moment and tried to emulate Tim's leadership style. At the time, I had no idea that within two years I would be in Tim's shoes playing against the best players from other schools and in a position to impact the other guys on the team. Tim's example gave me a vision for the future—and a standard to live up to—that I didn't forget.

In the fall of my sophomore year, Coach Cathrall started spending an inordinate amount of time working on my volleys. The main issue was my forehand—I always took the racket back too far and either missed the shot or hit the ball right to my opponent. As a result, I rarely, if ever, came to the net. After a week or two, I started to get not only frustrated but embarrassed as well. One afternoon, I left practice on the verge of tears. I was moping around my dorm floor that evening when my roommate yelled down the hall that Coach was on the phone (this was back when phones lived in one room and had cords). I remember my heart skipping a beat. To my knowledge, Coach had never called anyone in their dorm room. The only thing I could surmise was that he was either going to cut me from the team, or at the very least, move me down in the lineup. I picked up the phone reluctantly, bracing for the worst.

Coach said he had noticed how upset I was after practice but that he was spending so much time with me because he thought I was the best candidate to play number one the following year. I was speechless. I had never considered that possibility. But as I thought about it, it made sense. Tennis, back then, involved coming to the net quite often. Timmy McAvoy was an absolute beast at that; I'd never seen anyone better. But he would be graduating after that season, and unless we got an incredible recruit the following year, I would be a likely candidate to take his place. For that, I needed to become a better volleyer. Coach spent so much time with me because it was in the team's best interest, not because I was a hopeless tennis player. This was a major reframe for me, providing the confidence and vision that I sorely needed. To this day, that phone call in the dorm was as powerful as any I've ever received. No one other than Coach could have delivered such an impactful message. I've always been grateful for his belief in me—and I resolved not to let him down.

Good environments provide opportunities to learn from, and be inspired by, the example and encouragement of others.

Overload

Not too long after that phone call from Coach, I showed up for practice early. As usual, Timmy McAvoy was there too. He didn't say much—just walked on the court, grabbed a hopper of balls, and motioned for me to get ready to hit some volleys. Without warning or explanation, he hit a ball as hard as he could right at me from about thirty feet away. As the first ball whizzed past my head, he was already firing another. I quickly realized I needed to defend myself. My first instinct was to back up to allow more time to react. Something told me that would defeat the purpose. The only thing that would keep me from getting hit would be to *get my racket out in front to volley the ball.* Coach Cathrall had been telling me this for weeks; Tim got me to do it without saying a word.

Many years later, when I started coaching, I realized what had happened that day with Tim as I was reading Daniel Coyle's *The Talent Code.* Coyle describes a concept called "deep practice," which is "a zone of accelerated learning" where people "are purposely operating at the edges of their ability." Like a weightlifter increasing weight on the barbell, you have to "overload" the senses." As Coyle points out, world-class performers learn how to get comfortable practicing in this environment all the time. Tim firing balls at me was the embodiment of these principles. He decided to "overload" my volleys to get me to learn faster. I have no idea what inspired him to do it; most likely, he had picked up on Coach's vision, or maybe he was tired of me getting so much attention in practice. Whatever the reason, when Tim graduated, I played number one—and came to the net all the time.

The ultimate example of overload, on a bigger scale, was what Coach Cathrall called the "Southern Trip." This trip took place over spring break in late February and early March. I didn't have a clue what to expect my freshman year, but it didn't take long to figure out it wouldn't be a walk in the park. I hadn't looked at the schedule, so as we pulled away from Penn State, I asked one of the veteran players how long we'd be gone (hoping to return before the end of the school vacation). He looked at me and just shook his head.

As it turned out, we were scheduled to play eleven matches in eleven days, starting with the University of Virginia, which was five hours away. We would continue southward each day, arriving either the night before or the day of a match. We'd then play the match and move on to the next town. But that wasn't all. I soon came to discover that many of these matches would be played against some of the best college tennis programs in the country—Duke, UNC–Chapel Hill, Clemson, NC State, and the University of Georgia.

We traveled in a blue Ford Econovan provided by Penn State with Coach driving, our gear in the back row, and seven players packed in the middle. We spent a lot of time in that van. Now, when I see one like it on the road, I experience a weird form of PTSD with a crazy mix of associations—laughing while playing cards with my teammates, pouting in the back row after tough losses, smelling Bengay sports cream, listening to the Talking Heads or Jackson Browne (depending on my mood) on my Sony Walkman, and arguing about whether we'd eat lunch at Burger King, Wendy's, or McDonald's. That first year, for an eighteen-year-old freshman, it was a rude awakening. I got my ass kicked most every day by players who were stronger, more experienced, and mentally tougher than me. The only consolation was that my teammates were in the same boat.

The older guys explained that the Southern Trip was the brainchild of Coach Cathrall who, for many years, had been taking his teams on this trip to prepare for the official start of the season. The Southern Trip matches were not technically on our schedule. Since they were unofficial, the university did not cover expenses. Coach raised money during the off season to enable us to go, but those funds didn't go far. As a result, the trip was a bare-bones affair; we each got a small stipend for meals, usually stayed free in visiting team dormitories, and occasionally slept on the floors of fraternity houses. College tennis has long since established rules limiting the number of matches in a season, along with their prescribed duration, practice lengths, and so forth. But no such limits were in place during my college days. However, other than the damage to our psyches, I don't recall anyone on the team suffering anything worse than a muscle strain or the occasional cold. We quickly learned that, in Coach's mind, these conditions were not to be considered debilitating.

The goal for the spring break trip was to toughen us up. From that standpoint, Coach achieved his goal. During the regular season, we didn't face much we couldn't handle. And, I suppose, it prepared us for dealing with adversity in life after college. I remember driving home on the last leg of the Southern Trip during my senior year. I was talking with one of my best friends (and sometimes doubles partner) Jon Whiteside who, like me, hadn't missed a match in four seasons of playing for Coach Cathrall. We commented that the hardest thing we had done thus far in our lives, and one of our proudest accomplishments, was surviving four consecutive Southern Trips. Since we were starting to think about life after college, we wondered if perhaps our participation in these spring outings should be listed first on our resumés. We both laughed as we realized that, other than the guys on our team, no one would understand. But to this day, the Southern Trip is a common bond that unites all the guys who played for Coach Cathrall.

Playing under my college coach was a master class in how powerful overload can be in developing athletes (and people). It was also a lesson in leadership. Coach never asked us to do anything that he wasn't willing to do himself. During the time I was there, he was in his late fifties, yet he drove the same miles, slept on the same floors, ate the same food at McDonald's, fought through the same colds, and coached us against some of the best teams in the country. I think he had learned about overload long before we did—likely under much tougher conditions.

Environments that make you uncomfortable are the ones that lead to the most growth. Comfort is the enemy of progress.

Success

On my freshman Southern Trip, I was playing a tough match against a player who was unusually overbearing, arrogant, and contentious. I had limited experience playing guys like this, and when I did, I got intimidated, distracted, or both—and lost each time. But that day, something in me snapped. The match was close, and I felt myself getting more than a little pissed off with the guy. At one point, during a critical time in the match, I hit a running backhand passing shot past him at the net. As the shot went by, I muttered (although I didn't care if he heard me), "Take that, you son of a bitch."

I ended up right by the fence and, to my surprise, Coach was staring at me from five feet away. He didn't say a word, but the look on his face and the sly smile that emerged, said everything. He was telling me that if I was going to compete with the cockiest, toughest, and meanest opponents, then I would have to stand up for myself and, occasionally, bring those qualities out in myself. I could sense his pride and approval. Clearly, Coach was looking for players like me, and he knew he couldn't necessarily teach that type of competitive toughness. It was one thing to have the physical skills to play at this level (lots of guys did); it was quite another to have the psychological makeup required.

I don't remember if I won the match, which likely means I did, since I remember losses more than wins. But it really didn't matter. That moment with Coach was one of the most impactful I had in my college career. It taught me a subtle form of competitiveness that would be essential in the years to come playing similar opponents. Also, I think it earned me unspoken respect in Coach's eyes.

A few months later, in the fall of my sophomore year, the lessons I learned during that match came in handy. We were playing an invitational team event at the Naval Academy in Annapolis, Maryland. Many of the best teams in the Eastern United States were invited. Players from each team were put into one of three tournaments: the A flight was comprised of the top two players, the B flight was for the number three and four players, and the C flight was for the number five and six players. Each win counted as a point toward the overall team score. As the number three player for my team, I expected to play in the B flight. However, our number one player was injured so Coach put me in the A flight with the best players from the other teams. I felt like I was in over my head—as usual. But somehow, I kept winning and found myself playing in the finals.

My opponent was the hometown favorite, Navy's number one player. A crowd had already started to assemble as we took the court. As we warmed up, I heard the distinctive sound of marching in the distance getting louder as a group of Navy cadets, in full uniform, got closer. They marched in formation into the tennis center and took places sitting on a big concrete wall that overlooked the court. As we started playing the first game, they were cheering in a way that was, to my mind, clearly intended to distract and intimidate me. I could feel my anger boiling up inside. I knew I needed to toughen up and apply the lessons I had learned on the Southern Trip the previous spring. If I let them get under my skin, I'd be in big trouble. So, in my best John McEnroe imitation—loud, cocky, slightly obnoxious—I looked up and said, "Hey, could you guys keep it down up there?" I then avoided eye contact and channeled all my energy into playing the match. Before I knew it, I was at the net shaking hands with my opponent after a hard-fought win. That match established me, in the eyes of my teammates and our Coach, as a top player. But, more importantly, it gave me confidence in myself that was a springboard for the rest of my college career.

> *It's essential to occasionally have some success in challenging environments. Even small accomplishments can have a big impact.*

Process

For me, the "take that, you son of a bitch" moment with Coach and winning the Navy tournament were big credits in what I call the emotional bank account. Successes are credits; failures are debits. Of course, it's nice when you have more money coming in than going out. But sometimes the account balance can get too high. In my case, after I won that tournament at Navy, I started becoming overconfident. Basically, I was getting too big for my britches. By my junior year, I expected to play well in every practice during the week and win *all* my matches on the weekends. When that didn't happen, which was often, I went into what Coach Cathrall dubbed "the blue funk"—I moped, whined, pouted, or acted out.

In one embarrassing moment, I broke a racket on a net post after losing a close match in front of a home crowd at Penn State. In another, I picked a fight with some players from Yale who, in my opinion, had disrespected my doubles partner by hitting him with a ball. (FYI, fighting in college tennis doesn't get physical. It involves a lot of swearing, tough guy looks, and an occasional shot intended to hit other players.) In a match against Rutgers, I questioned the integrity of an umpire from New Jersey after he ruled against me in a line call dispute, based solely on the fact that he was from the same state as my opponent. In short, I was becoming a typical self-absorbed tennis brat.

This all came to a head on another trip to the Naval Academy when I accidentally overheard Navy's pre-match team meeting before a dual match. The topic was how to deal with *my* behavior and attitude. Apparently, I was known to be overly feisty on the court, prone to constantly questioning line calls, acting slightly arrogant, and being a general pain in the ass. Their coach was alerting his players to anticipate but not get distracted by my antics. My dad's term for this was, "Don't get into a pissing match with a skunk." In this case, I was the skunk. This was embarrassing because I had the utmost respect for the whole program at Navy—they had one of the best coaches in the country (Bob Bayliss), and their players had a unique blend of camaraderie, competitiveness, toughness, and sportsmanship. That moment impacted me more than any lecture a coach could have given. I realized I needed to take a hard look at how I conducted myself and make some changes.

By senior year, I had finally found the right balance between competitiveness and humility—and, hopefully, I had earned back the respect of the guys at Navy. It took time to learn how to keep success and failure in perspective. That was precisely what Timmy McAvoy had modeled for me as a freshman. But at the time, I didn't know how important this balance was, nor how to attain it. I now understand that it was a four-year process that couldn't be rushed—and that the college environment was uniquely suited for my development as an athlete, not to mention my growth as a human being.

The best environments enable you to develop over time. There are no shortcuts, and failure is part of the process.

CHAPTER 4
PROFESSIONALISM

During the spring of my senior year, most of my peers were thinking about the traditional post-college pursuits—jobs and grad school, for example. But my heart was still on the tennis court. I wanted to play professionally and test myself against the best players. Of course, this was just a dream. I had no idea what it took or where to start—nor how hard and humbling it would turn out to be.

Higher Standards

In another example of "who" luck (like meeting Terry McMahon in my early teens), I met a tennis coach named Peter Daub during Christmas break of my senior year. I was playing a men's tournament at a club he owned just outside of Philadelphia. Since the tournament offered prize money, it attracted a slew of strong players. Many college players entered in hopes of getting good competition even though, as amateurs, we couldn't accept any money. I found myself in the semifinals playing the top player for Columbia University. We had a great match which I ended up winning in a close third set. I thought I had played well and was feeling quite good about myself. As I walked toward the locker room, I graciously received praise from people who had watched the match—like a member of the royal family waving to the crowd. This inflated my ego even more.

As I emerged from the shower, still basking in the glow of my great match, a "coach-y" looking guy with a serious demeanor appeared, clipboard in hand. He introduced himself as Peter Daub and said he was a tennis coach at the club. He had heard I was considering playing professionally and asked if I might be interested in some coaching feedback related to that goal. I assumed that compliments would surely be forthcoming. I told Mr. Daub I'd be happy to hear what he had to say. I did notice, however, that he had a full page of notes on his clipboard. To my surprise, every bullet point addressed an area in which I could improve. As he reviewed each one, I felt both confused and curious. I could tell he was talking about tennis; I just didn't understand much of what he was saying. No one had ever spoken about tennis to me with such directness, substance, and authority. Even though it didn't all make sense; I got the impression Coach Daub knew what he was talking about. This guy was unlike any coach I'd ever met. We parted ways, with my ego now thoroughly in check.

In January, back at school, a letter arrived from Peter Daub. He offered to coach me and outlined a long list of things I needed to add to my training if I wanted to pursue professional tennis: running a mile in a certain amount of time, hitting serves for various targets, and so on. I hadn't considered that I'd need to do more than what I was doing at the college level to play professionally. Clearly, Coach Daub had entered the picture at the perfect time. I replied that I'd do my best to implement his suggestions and would love for him to coach me after I graduated.

Professionalism is about establishing—and attaining— the highest of standards. In most cases, they will be far beyond the standards you currently hold.

Different Mindsets

When I arrived at Coach Daub's club for our first practice the following June, I was looking forward to embarking on a new journey. I had arrived right on time, but it looked as if Coach Daub had already been on the court for a while preparing for our session. He hadn't said a word yet, but I could tell things were going to be much different under his tutelage.

I swung the gate open and bounded onto the court like a puppy at the dog park. Coach Daub now spoke. He told me to turn around and walk back out. He walked over and explained, from the other side of the fence, that from that point forward I was to consider myself a professional tennis player. Therefore, I should never walk onto a tennis court without first reminding myself that it was my place of business. As a professional, I needed to arrive early each day ready to give my undivided attention. Anything outside the court needed to be left behind, and he would accept nothing but my full effort. Once I acknowledged all this, he allowed me to walk back through the gate. This brought back memories of our initial meeting. I didn't quite understand what he was saying or why, but I sensed it was in my best interest to listen——and do whatever he said.

Coach Daub explained early in our relationship that he wouldn't be taking credit for my wins, nor accepting blame for my losses. As usual, I didn't get why he made a point of this. Much later, I understood that he was teaching me about personal accountability. In college, athletes have a big support system—coaches, trainers, free equipment, food, transportation, and so on. You get used to these comforts and tend to take them for granted. But once you turn pro, you are responsible for everything. There's no safety net for when things go wrong, and no one *gives* you anything in pro tennis. Coach Daub wanted me to understand this from the start. He'd always be there for me, but when things were the toughest, I'd likely be somewhere far away from his direct oversight. This turned out to be true in ways I couldn't imagine (see Chapter 7).

I tried to embrace these new concepts, and for the most part, I did a good job. But I always had in the back of my mind that if pro tennis didn't work out, I'd apply to graduate school and continue my education. This seemed like a reasonable fallback position. I mentioned this often to Coach Daub when things weren't going well on the tennis court. About six months after we started working together, I was playing another tournament at his club against Scott Nichol, who had consistently beaten me in the past. Like me, Scott had just graduated from college and was starting to play pro events. He was a real force on the tennis court, aggressive in every way. Although I had the skills to compete with Scott, he intimidated me mentally and overpowered me physically. This match was no different than our others—I lost badly.

I came off the court dejected and headed for the locker room. Coach Daub met me there to review the match. As was typical when things went badly, I started our discussion by mentioning my fallback position of heading to graduate school. Coach stopped me mid-sentence and said in no uncertain terms, "Bill, if you want to go to grad school . . . GO TO GRAD SCHOOL, but if you want to play tennis, PLAY TENNIS!" He made it clear that either option was fine with him, but if I decided to play tennis, he didn't want to hear one more word about grad school. To this day, forty years later, whenever we talk about our few years together as coach and student, he mentions that moment as the most pivotal in my pro tennis journey. That's because he knew I was hedging my bet with grad school and hadn't completely committed to pro tennis. To even have a chance of success, I needed to jump off the diving board. If I didn't want to do that, I needed to climb back down the ladder and move on with life. I needed someone to force me to make that decision. Fortunately, Coach Daub was the perfect person for the job because he was always direct, honest, and willing to tell me what I needed to hear. I played pro tennis for another year and a half, put graduate school on the back burner, and never mentioned it again.

Professionalism involves changing old habits and patterns of thought. It's a lifestyle that takes total commitment.

Key Principles

Once I established the right mindset, the question became: what do I need to learn on the court? In other words, what specific principles did I need to cultivate to be successful? As I started my journey from college to pro tennis with Coach Daub, this was where things got interesting. I'd played four years of Division 1 college tennis, yet it was amazing how little I knew about playing the sport well.

We started with learning how I needed to manage mistakes. In college, I thought mistakes were to be avoided at all costs because it meant losing the point. But I learned from Coach Daub that mistakes are part of the game, and you don't need to beat yourself up every time you make one. However, you do need to pay ruthless attention to making corrections. Since I was usually worked up over losing the point, I rarely paid attention to correcting on the next shot. As a result, I tended to repeat the same mistakes. Here's the basic idea behind this concept.

There are only four ways you can miss your target in tennis—short, long, right, or left. Coach Daub taught me to observe where I had just missed (without judgment!), visualize where I'd like the ball to go next time, and move on. The goal was not to miss that same way twice. If I'd missed the last shot long, I needed to hit lower on the next shot; if I'd missed too far right, I needed to hit the next shot left. It wasn't about telling myself *how* to do that—it was about paying attention and visualizing *where* I wanted the next ball to go, then trusting my body to do it when the time came. When the chatter of self-criticism cluttered my mind, it interfered with my body's ability to perform. My body already knew how to execute; I just needed to get out of the way.

As I soon learned after reading books like the *Inner Game of Tennis*,[8] this was a foundational principle of sports psychology. The only time Coach Daub would correct me was when I had "checked out" mentally and made the same error two times in a row. Anyone who's ever watched pro tennis knows that the best players rarely, if ever, allow that to happen. I needed to develop a different—and better—mental habit if I wanted to compete with the best.

Another paradigm shift was in how I thought about visualizing targets. One day, early in our time together on the court, I hit a ball into the net. Coach Daub came over and asked, as if the answer was obvious, "What is the primary target in tennis?" Not knowing what to say, I think I answered, "Hit the ball away from your opponent." He proceeded to explain that, while it was fine to hit the ball away from your opponent, in tennis I should focus on only two targets. The first was what he called the "primary" target—the net. For a ball to go in the opponent's court, it must first *go over the net*. Having watched me play, he had observed that half the errors I made were into the net. Therefore, by learning to clear the net, I would cut my errors by 50 percent. As obvious as this was, it was a revelation to me. I was so busy trying to run my opponent around that I hadn't noticed how many balls I hit into the net.

---

8 Tim Gallwey presents this idea in *The Inner Game of Tennis* through the concepts of the "self 1," which is constantly talking and evaluating, and the "self 2," which is fully capable of executing without obsessive oversight and instruction. For a more current take on this theme, I recommend *The Mindful Athlete* by George Mumford.

But Coach Daub wasn't finished. He pointed out that clearing the primary target was just step one in the process. Step two was deciding where the "secondary" target was. For that, I had two choices—both located about six feet from the corners of my opponent's court. I usually aimed much closer to the lines, but secondary targets allowed more margin for error and, as a result, I made fewer mistakes. From that point on, we always practiced with two big yellow cones marking the secondary targets. Whenever I hit a tennis ball, I first visualized the ball going over the net and then which secondary target I wanted to hit. This may sound simple, but for me it was a completely different way of playing tennis, and it resulted in my becoming a more consistent, effective player.

Like any good teacher, Coach Daub knew how to build on what he taught. Once I had the basic idea of primary/secondary targets down, he introduced a related but more advanced concept called risk factors. Anything that increases your odds of missing a shot is a risk factor. As I mentioned earlier, my idea of tennis was to run my opponent around and, hopefully, hit winners as often as possible. This meant I needed to do quite a few things:

- Hit hard.

- Hit low over the net.

- Hit close to the lines.

- Hit deep.

- Hit early ("on the rise," just as the ball came off the court, from preferably near, or inside, my own baseline).

- Change direction often (if the guy hit the ball crosscourt, I would hit it down the line, and vice versa).

There is no debate that these things increase the likelihood of winning points. My mistake was in assuming that, with practice, *I could take all these risks at the same time while never making errors.* I thought that's what it would take to compete in pro tennis. Coach Daub made it clear that this simply wasn't possible, even for the best players in the world. He explained that pro players rarely take more than *one risk factor at a time.* The game wasn't about hitting more winners; it was about making fewer errors. Therefore, it would be okay if I didn't hurt my opponent every single time I hit the ball. Sometimes I simply needed to give the opponent the opportunity to miss. This, ironically, is what I realized my opponents were doing when they played me. They didn't mind if I hit one winner if, in the effort to do that, I made two errors.

This meant I needed to adopt two new rules. First, if I was on the run or off balance, then I would choose a high percentage shot and *get the ball in play* (over the net and to a secondary target). Second, if I was in position and wanted to take some risk, then I would *only take one risk at a time.* If I wanted to hit the ball harder, then I shouldn't aim close to the line. If I wanted to hit closer to a line, I shouldn't hit it harder. It took a relatively short period of time to incorporate these principles once I realized that errors by my opponent were worth the same number of points as winners. Believe it or not, this too was a revelation to me.

To develop professionally, you need core principles that form the basis for how you train. The concepts may be simple, but the execution will take time and effort.

Mental Skills

By the time I got a year into training with Coach Daub, I had improved significantly from a physical standpoint. However, the mental aspect is what sets apart good players from great ones. That was the missing puzzle piece in my game. I tended to be overly self-critical, had trouble staying focused, and lacked confidence. No matter how good I got in practice, I'd get derailed during competition. Therefore, Coach Daub felt it would be helpful to get some advice from sports psychologists.

He first referred me to Dr. Jim Loehr in Denver, Colorado. Although I didn't know it at the time, Dr. Loehr would become one of the leading sports psychologists in the world. I think he charged six hundred dollars a day, which I would consider a bargain today. But since I had to fly to Denver and put myself up, this was no small investment for a guy barely scraping by in the minor leagues of pro tennis. Dr. Loehr met me at the airport in the morning and took me to a tennis club. He had arranged for a local pro to play a set against me while he recorded the session on video.

We went back to his office and meticulously reviewed the tape. He paid no attention to technique, tactics, footwork, or the outcome of the set. Instead, he focused on my body language and physical presence: how I carried my racket, how I walked, what I did between points, and so on. He then played videos of some of the best players in the world. They looked composed, confident, and clear about what they were doing. I tended to rush around the court looking distracted, listless, and unsure of myself. This reflected the unconscious habits of thought I had accumulated over many years.

As we finished reviewing the tapes, Dr. Loehr explained that many tools were available to help me improve, but there were no quick fixes. It would take time and practice, just like everything else I had done in sports. The main purpose would be to enable me to access what he called the "ideal performance state" (IPS) more readily and consistently. Dr. Loehr, I believe, was the first to use this term to describe the mental and physiological states associated with peak athletic performance. It's used widely today, as any quick internet search will reveal. I left Denver with one of Dr. Loehr's books and lots of homework involving visualization, breathing techniques, and body awareness exercises.

When I returned from that trip, Coach Daub connected me with another sports psychologist named Dr. Glenn White. His emphasis was on developing rituals between points. I could easily see the relationship between this and attaining the IPS. The first thing Dr. White explained was that I shouldn't feel guilty about having extraneous thoughts during competition. This was a relief. I had always assumed that the crazy thoughts running through my head while I played were a sign of weakness. Dr. White told me they were normal and to be expected. The key to staying focused, relaxed, and confident was simply to take more time between points if my mind was racing, as I tended to rush between points. The rituals he taught forced me to slow down. They gave me the time I needed to clear my mind of distracting thoughts and visualize what I wanted to do next.

Some examples of these rituals:

- Gently roll a ball to the side of the court and walk over slowly to pick it up.

- Position a towel at the back fence and take your time getting to it.

- Bounce the ball numerous times before serving.

- Turn your back to your opponent before returning serve until you're ready to play the next point.

- Take your time straightening the strings on your racquet.

Anyone who watches pro tennis on TV will see techniques like these used regularly. After a few weeks of practice, I traveled to a circuit in Texas where I had played the two previous years with little success. That year, using what Dr. Loehr and Dr. White had taught me, I had the best results of my pro career. There was no question that the improvement in my mental game had made all the difference.

At the professional level, mental skills are essential. To improve in that area, you need specific tools—and a commitment to practicing them.

CHAPTER 5
HUMILITY

I spent two years traveling the world playing pro tennis—I had some amazing experiences and met some great people. But none of that would have happened without the support of my parents. When I started out, my dad offered to form a corporation with me called Schillings Enterprises. Any money I made playing or teaching went in, all my expenses came out, and my parents agreed to fund any shortfall. There was just one provision: if the corporation was running at a loss after two years, then the agreement would dissolve. At the end of two years, the numbers didn't add up, and I had to face the fact that, no matter how determined I was, I wouldn't make it as a professional tennis player. I assumed that after leaving the pro circuit, I'd move into the real world of conventional work (whatever that meant). As it turned out, I was just embarking on my career in tennis—and still had much to learn.

Trying Less, Trusting More

Once again, in what the writer Maria Popova calls a "baffling blur of time and chance,"[9] the right people came along at the right time. Peter Daub, who had been coaching me for the previous two years, had just become the head tennis coach at Temple University. He offered me a position as his assistant, coaching the men's and women's teams. In exchange, I could go to graduate school for free. It didn't take long for me to say yes to that.

While doing research for my master's thesis on sports psychology, I came across a concept called the "inverted U hypothesis" (fancy name, simple idea). It explained in graph form the relationship between performance and intensity in sports. The idea was that beyond a certain level of intensity, performance drops. In other words, it's possible to try too hard. And while that may seem obvious to some, I realized I'd never understood this as a player. I'd grown up steeped in the idea that the harder you try, the better you perform. So, when I wasn't performing well, I tried to play better by force of will. This rarely had any positive effect. If anything, it usually made things worse.

The inverted U hypothesis explained that to perform your best, you must find a balance between relaxation and effort . . .

9 themarginalian.org/2022/10/23/16-learnings/

sometimes it's better to trust more, not try harder. I had never thought about it this way before, although it was exactly what the sports psychologists had been telling me all along (with terms like "calm intensity," "getting in the zone," and "ideal performance state"). The visual of that inverted U graph enabled me to finally understand. It was humbling to realize how little I had grasped about the psychology of sports when I was competing professionally. Fortunately, however, I would have more opportunities to put this concept into practice.

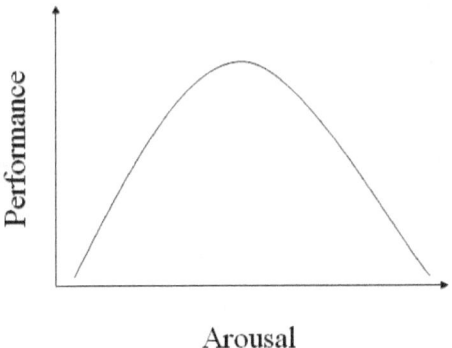

The 'inverted U' theory proposes that sporting performance improves as arousal levels increase but that there is a threshold point. Any increase in arousal beyond the threshold point will worsen performance. At low arousal levels, performance quality is low. This visual resulted in an 'aha' moment for me; trying harder doesn't always mean playing better.

You don't always achieve success by "making" it happen.
Sometimes it's better to "let" it happen—
there's a big difference.

Paying My Dues

While in grad school, I played in a national tournament at the International Tennis Hall of Fame in Newport, Rhode Island. Only sixteen players qualified from around the country, so after winning my first round, I was already in the quarterfinals. My opponent was Juan Nunez, a former touring pro who had been ranked in the top 200 in the world. Even though I had just spent two years in the minor leagues of pro tennis, this would be the highest ranked player I'd ever played—and more money than I had ever played for.

After a long battle, I had two match points as I prepared to return serve at 4–5, 15–40 in the third set. I reminded myself to do what Coach Daub had always preached in those situations—get the ball in play, make the guy hit, clear the net, aim for a secondary target, and so on. To my credit, I did exactly that. But Juan was used to situations like this. He hit winners on both points and used that momentum to win the next two points easily. The score was now 5–5, which wasn't a bad place to be. I still had a good chance to win, but I couldn't seem to let go of those lost match points. My mind bounced between the past, those lost match points, and the future—the possibility of still winning the match. Somehow the task at hand, playing the points as they came, got lost in the shuffle. I made a few unforced errors in the next two games, lost them quickly, and the next thing I knew, I was shaking hands with Juan and walking off the court wondering what had just happened.

My girlfriend, Liz, still new to the nuances of the sport, awaited me after the match. The following brief conversation ensued.

"Did you know that you had two match points?" Liz asked.

"Ahh, yes . . . I did know that. Thanks," I replied.

Liz later realized that the timing of her comment hadn't been ideal. Nevertheless, I married her the next year. We joke about it these days. Back then, I hadn't thought it was so funny.

A few years later, I found myself in a similar situation. This time the opponent was Tim Wilkison, who had been ranked in the top 100 in the world for many years. I had practiced with him a few times, so the intimidation factor had worn off somewhat, but I knew going in that he was the better player. I started the match playing well and found myself up in the first set 4–1. Having learned from experience playing Juan, I reminded myself to stay focused and present-centered. However, as Tim started serving the next game, I noticed he seemed to be taking *forever* between points. He would go back and towel off first, then go through an elaborate ritual before every serve or return. In my mind, this was clearly designed to throw me off my game. I got distracted as my frustration built with every point. The momentum shifted, and Tim won the next five games, winning the set 6–4.

When you're competing against a player at his level, once you lose a lead, it's hard to get it back, so the second set went quickly in Tim's favor as well. After the match, looking for justification, I asked a friend if he'd seen how shamelessly Tim had tried to throw me off. He said Tim had never gone over the time allotted in the rules and, more importantly, I needed to be tougher mentally in pressure situations like that. I thought, *Some friend he turned out to be.* Sometimes it's hard to hear the truth.

Of course, my friend was right. In the matches against Juan and Tim, I'd allowed myself to go beyond the peak of the curve on the inverted U graph. My emotions ran the show (as Dr. Loehr liked to say), and my performance dropped. I understood this concept well having studied it in school, but there was still a gap between the theory and my ability to execute. Clearly, both Juan and Tim were more competitively savvy than I was; they'd paid their dues by playing more high-level matches than I had. I doubt either one had heard of the inverted U hypothesis, but they certainly embodied what it taught. They knew how to control their emotions under pressure. The only way to get to their level would be to pay my dues as well—there were no shortcuts I could take.

There's a difference between theory and practice. The only way to bridge that gap is through experience—and we often learn the most when things don't go our way.

Mid-match on the grass courts at the Tennis Hall of Fame
in Newport, Rhode Island.

Turning Things Around

As humbling as these matches against top players were, I
continued to play tournaments and apply what I had learned
in those tough losses. Fortunately, a few times, things worked
out. One was a match I played against Mike Pittard, who had
just won the North Carolina State Championships. Before the
match, a well-meaning friend sought me out to alert me to how
strong a player Mike was. He made it sound as if I was about

to embark on a journey through the desert without any water. Regardless of his good intentions, I had learned to block information like that out of my head. Nothing good could come from losing the match before it started. I must admit, however, that when we started warming up, I could see what my friend was talking about. Immediately, I could feel the power of Mike's groundstrokes and serve. When the match began, he aced me on at least half the points he served. And any shot that I didn't hit with pace and depth, he attacked and won the point easily. I wondered why this guy wasn't on the pro tour.

But then, as many of my coaches had told me, I remembered to focus on "controlling what I could control." I needed only to concern myself with how well I played, not with how good Mike seemed to be. As my mind cleared and we got further into the match, I noticed that Mike didn't move quite as well as I did. He preferred coming to the net and ending points quickly to playing long points at the baseline. If I could get him into longer points, I knew my odds would improve. I was able to do this on my service games, which I barely won, but Mike easily won his service games using his big serve to set up shorter points . . . until he was serving at 4–5. In that game, likely due to the pressure of the moment, Mike missed most of his first serves.

Up to that point, I'd never gotten more than one or two points during his service games; now I found myself up a set point at 30–40. I tried to focus on the fundamentals—stay in the moment, and if I could touch the ball . . . *get it in the court.* He hit a big serve that I barely got my racket on. My return floated softly over the net. It looked like Mike would routinely hit a volley winner . . . but he dumped it right into the middle of the net. It seemed as if I had been barely competitive the entire time, so I couldn't believe I'd won the set.

As we sat down at the changeover, I wondered how I'd be able to win another set. It had taken more mental stamina to win one set against Mike than it did playing three sets against other players. But to my surprise, the second set was nearly identical to the first. I barely won any points in his service games. I won my service games with great difficulty, and once again, had one break point at 4–4 in which he missed an easy volley. I then held serve to win 6–4, 6–4. Mentally, it felt as if I had survived a war of attrition—I'd lost a lot of troops but had just enough reinforcements to come up with the win. If we had gone three sets, I doubt I would have been able to keep playing at that level. I had a headache from concentrating for so long and sat for a while waiting for it to go away. After losing many matches due to cracks in my psychological armor, it was gratifying to know I had held up well in this one. The headache was a small price to pay for that feeling of satisfaction.

Pay your dues, and sooner or later you'll reap rewards.
The harder the struggle, the higher the satisfaction.

Process Before Outcome

In 1987, I got my first tennis teaching job in Charlotte at Olde Providence Racquet Club. Every year back then, they held a pro exhibition tournament. Many of the top players in the world were invited. Some were veterans, but some rising stars also participated, like Andre Agassi and Pete Sampras. The week before one event, the tournament director asked if I could practice with Michael Chang, one of the players. I asked around and found that the sixteen-year-old Chang had just turned pro. I was twenty-seven, and I couldn't picture him being much of a threat on the tennis court.

My first impression was that he looked fit but not too physically imposing. He was shy, wordlessly nodding without making eye contact when we were introduced. His entourage consisted of his mom (omnipresent, never taking her eyes off Michael) and his coach (a quiet, intense-looking guy). Few words were spoken by anyone, so I figured it best to go with the flow and do what I was told.

We started to warm up by hitting straight ahead. The kid may have been young, but he sure could hit groundstrokes . . . and he *never* missed. Also, he hit hard. I couldn't figure out where all that power was coming from. When he took off his warmup pants, that question was answered. He may have been small in stature, but he was strong as an ox—his legs looked like tree trunks. I realized that playing this kid might require my full attention.

I hit a few balls away from him just to see what would happen. Michael was quick, to put it mildly—like his body was spring-loaded and ready to explode for every ball hit in his direction. I noticed that his coach required him to run down balls even when I'd hit them outside the court, and he did this effortlessly. It struck me that playing him from the baseline might not be all that pleasant. As that thought solidified, Michael's coach said that he wanted us to play a set. I prepared for the worst but resolved to give my best effort.

Just before the first point, I saw his coach say something to him quietly, which Michael acknowledged without saying a word. As the set started, I noticed he was coming to the net every point. I could only assume that's what his coach had told him to do. This didn't make sense. Michael was great at the baseline but didn't volley all that well. I was usually able to pass him outright, because of his shorter reach, or force errors due to his weak volleys. I won the set but couldn't understand why Michael hadn't stayed at the baseline where he would have beaten me easily.

When we finished, everyone packed up and left. I received an eerie gaze from Michael's mom and a quiet stare from his coach; it was . . . weird. I didn't think much more about that practice session until the next summer when I turned on my TV. There was Michael Chang, running all over the court beating Ivan Lendl (the number one player in the world) in the fourth round of the French Open before going on to win the tournament. This was insane; the kid was only seventeen years old.[10] But what really surprised me was how much his volleys had improved.

Then it hit me. When we had practiced at Olde Providence, Michael's coach knew he would have killed me from the baseline. Michael needed to improve his volleys if he wanted to be competitive with the world's best. The way to accomplish that was to play lower-level players like me in practice and come to the net. That coach may have been mysterious, but he knew what he was doing. It didn't matter if Michael won or lost a practice set—what mattered was that he got better at tennis. And even though Michael won the French Open that year due to his baseline game, it certainly didn't hurt that he could volley well.

I have yet to receive a thank you card for practicing with Michael that day. My wife still likes to tell people at parties that I once beat him in a practice set. I suppose she thinks that may impress someone. Clearly, however, a few mitigating circumstances may have diminished that accomplishment.

Don't let your ego dictate how you practice.
Focus on improvement and the results will follow.

10 https://www.youtube.com/watch?v=u0NkCiZsAJ4

Channeling the Right Energy

The pro exhibitions at Olde Providence had eight players from the pro tour. To stir up interest, the organizers selected eight local players with some experience playing college and/or pro tennis, then paired them with a touring pro to play in the doubles event. One year I played with a promising 18-year-old named Jim Courier. He seemed like a nice, easygoing kid—no different than many of the teenagers I taught at the club . . . until I saw him hit a tennis ball.

Our first match was in front of a good crowd who had shown up early to watch a singles match featuring Andre Agassi (another teenager, then ranked in the world's top ten, who had recently taken the tennis world by storm). As we took to the court, I could feel the butterflies in my stomach. I glanced over at Jim; he didn't seem to have a care in the world. I hoped he had some game since our opponents were Richey Reneberg, a tour veteran, and Pender Murphy, a former all-American at Clemson and top 100 tour pro.

Early in the match, Richey was about to serve to Jim for the first time. As Jim walked past me to return serve, he stopped by and said with a sly, fun-loving smile on his face, "I'm gonna hit the crap out of this ball!" Then he marched back to the baseline. This struck me as peculiar since I had never once thought to "hit the crap out of a ball" in preparation for returning the serve of a world-class pro. Richey hit a decent serve wide to Jim's backhand. Jim's feet came to life. He was a big kid and I had no idea he could move so well. Within a split second, he had run around his backhand and hit the biggest forehand I had ever seen or heard—it sounded like a gun going off. It came back so quickly that Richey had no chance to touch the ball. Fortunately for him, it sailed just out. A brief, stunned silence fell over the stands. I doubt anyone else had seen a forehand like that before either. Jim glanced over at me with that same sly smile. He was enjoying himself and clearly unconcerned about losing the point.

I don't remember what happened on the next point when Richey served to me; I was too busy thinking about what Jim was going to do on his next return. Sure enough, he ran around his backhand again and hit that same forehand. This time it was directed straight at Pender's head, who was standing just a few feet away at the net. Pender ducked to avoid being decapitated by the ball. This time the shot landed in, and we won the point. I had no idea there were people in the world who could hit a tennis ball that hard, especially eighteen-year-olds. And win or lose, Jim never backed off his shots. He exuded a unique blend of confidence, competitiveness, and youthful exuberance that I'd never seen before.

As it turned out, Jim and I were the perfect doubles combination. I was the solid, consistent guy, while he was the bold, go-for-broke guy. And since his forehands went in often, we won our first two matches and made it to the finals. Our opponents were Luke Jensen, who in a few years would go on to win the French Open with his brother Murphy, and Mike Gandolfo, another former all-American at Clemson and top doubles player on the tour. The stands were full of spectators in anticipation of the singles final after our match, and I felt a now-familiar nervousness as we took the court. Jim, as usual, seemed unaffected. By this time, even though he was ten years younger than me, I looked to him to set the tone psychologically. I tried to channel his energy and enjoy the moment.

Me and Jim Courier warming up for the final.

The match was a blur until I was about to serve at 6–4, 5–4. Thoughts racing, nerves rising, I was at the baseline trying to calm myself when I noticed Jim walking toward me from his position at the net. With a smile on his face, he looked me in the eyes and said, "Hey, let's take this thing home!" It was the perfect thing to say. I could feel the confidence in his voice, and it rubbed off. We won the tournament, and it became one of my most memorable moments in tennis. I have no doubt Jim moved on within minutes, and that's okay, because we all have our own paths to walk. As it turned out, Jim's path took him quite far. Within a few years, he had won multiple Grand Slams and become the number one player in the world. It all started with that big win in Charlotte playing exhibition doubles with me. At least, that's my version of the story . . . and I'm sticking to it.

Don't take yourself too seriously—learn how to have fun, especially in high-pressure, competitive environments.

PART II
STORIES

CHAPTER 6
MATCH PREPARATION

When Coach Daub began to coach me in my professional career, he knew that I'd need to improve my skills to the point where I didn't have to "think" when under pressure in competition. In other words, to have the best chance to win matches, I needed to become "unconsciously competent"—physically, technically, tactically, and psychologically. This is a construct, or pyramid, of learning that has been invaluable to me as a player, coach, and parent.

There are four levels:

- unconscious incompetence (you're incompetent, but you don't know it);

- conscious incompetence (you're aware that you're incompetent, but still not very good);

- conscious competence (you're competent, but only with intention and effort);

- unconscious competence (you're competent without intention and effort).

To this end, I needed plenty of purposeful, consistent, disciplined practice. That didn't mean that I needed to do anything fancy. Coach Daub would simply set a standard beyond my current skill level, design a corresponding drill, and then require me to practice until I achieved that level. But unfortunately, simple doesn't always mean easy.

Fitness

One of Coach Daub's fitness standards was for me to be able to run two miles in under twelve minutes. I was a tennis player, not a track star, so that one took quite some time. Another one was my personal favorite, the four-ball drill. This involved placing four balls between the baseline and the net, equally spaced along the sideline in seven-foot intervals. Standing at the baseline and starting with the ball closest to you, you pick up each ball, place it at the baseline, and then return all four balls to their original positions. The standard was thirty seconds with thirty seconds to recover. If I finished the drill in thirty seconds, I "earned" the right to do another, with the goal of completing ten rounds. Achieving that goal was the single most physically challenging thing I've ever done. I think it took me the better part of a year to conquer it. Try it sometime. Although, unless you are in amazing shape, I suggest you lower the standard.

Consistency

When it came to technical development, Coach Daub would pick something I needed to be good at—let's say consistent groundstrokes. The first progression might be to hit fifty balls in a row with a practice partner at moderate pace. If we could do that, we'd divide the court in half and be required to hit the ball crosscourt and down the line. This would force both players to run for every ball and hit smaller targets, all the while maintaining the fifty-ball consistency standard. Whenever we achieved one goal, the constraints would be modified to make things more challenging (either with accuracy, consistency, or pace). This sounds a lot easier on paper than it is in practice. Each new version of a drill might take weeks or months to master.

Depth

One of the many things I needed to improve upon was hitting groundstrokes deeper. To work on this, Coach Daub put a line of cones six feet from my opponent's baseline. Hitting the ball in that zone meant I had hit an effective, deep shot. When we started, I was insanely bad at this. In my college days, this would have made me crazy. But now, using the concept of corrections he'd taught me when we first started working together, all I had to do was not miss the same way twice. I rarely got frustrated and, to my amazement, in a short time I was consistently able to execute that skill with unconscious competence. Once I started playing pro tennis matches, I realized how important that was. You don't have the luxury of missing a shot and correcting in matches, so you better get so good in practice that you rarely miss.

Serve Effectiveness

We worked on serving by blocking off small zones, two feet wide, in each service box (one in each corner and one right down the middle), and I'd hit ten serves for each zone (total of sixty serves) five or six days a week. I was required to record how many serves of the ten I made to each zone. When I first started this drill, my average was two or three. After a year, I could regularly hit seven or eight. At the pro level, many players are consistently able to hit these small zones at high speeds, which results in what we call free points—hitting only one serve to win the point. One day, Coach Daub asked me, "How much would you pay in a pro match for one free point per game? I understood his logic: I loved free points in matches, but the only way to get them was to spend hours hitting those targets in practice.

Transition

Some of the most impactful drills we did were transition drills. These had to do with attacking and coming to the net or defending against your opponent doing the same. My mindset in college had been to hit my first shot so well that I would win the point outright, regardless of whether I was attacking or defending. Notice a recurring theme—ending the point quickly by taking lots of risks. This resulted in lots of errors but, in my egocentric mind, if my opponent never got to hit winners, the tradeoff would be worth it.

One day during practice, Coach Daub asked: "What is the percentage of first shots you should make when attacking or defending?" After an awkward silence, he supplied the answer—100 percent. How might that be possible? If your purpose is to end the point in one shot, then it isn't. But if you are using primary and secondary targets, are aware of risk factors, and are okay with allowing your opponent to hit the ball, then 100 percent should be the standard—at least according to Coach Daub.

The drill he used to teach this involved feeding a short ball to my practice partner and having him attack. I had only one objective, regardless of where the opponent was, which was to hit the ball over the primary target to a secondary target. The same would be true if I was attacking. It didn't matter what happened next. In Coach Daub's eyes, I was successful if I made my first shot. Occasionally, my practice partner would hit a winning volley or passing shot. Initially, this really bothered me. But it was all part of the plan. The purpose was to de-condition me from the fear of my opponent hitting winners, teach me to aim for targets I could hit consistently, and to make fewer errors. To do that, I would sometimes have to hit "through" my opponent, not "around" them. After I bought into this premise and practiced transition drills for many hours, I found that whenever I was attacking or defending in a match, time slowed down, I knew exactly what I was going to do—and I rarely missed.

The payoff from all this training, particularly those transition drills, came during the most pressure-packed moment I'd ever had on a tennis court. I was playing Scott Nichols, who had beaten me soundly every time we'd played. We were in the finals of a regional tournament sponsored by Reebok. The winner would receive five hundred dollars and an all-expense paid trip to a national event at the International Tennis Hall of Fame, where bigger prize money was guaranteed. This was, at the time, the most money I had ever played for.

After close to three hours, I found myself at match point needing just one more point to win. My palms were sweating, my breathing was weak, and I could feel my heart beating. Scott hit a serve, attacked, and positioned himself perfectly at the net. All the things Coach Daub had ingrained in me kicked in—clear the primary target, aim for a secondary target, hit through the guy, don't worry about him hitting a winner. I put my head down, trusted myself, and hit the ball down the line. When I looked up, I saw that Scott had guessed crosscourt. You could have driven a Mack truck through that open space. The ball seemed to take forever to land, but land it did—right where the secondary target would have been on Coach Daub's practice court. The prize money was nice, but it's long gone. That memory, however, has never faded—it was one of the best feelings I've ever had on a tennis court.

Pop's Advice

Years after I'd left the professional circuit and was well into my career as a coach, I found a treasure buried in a file: five stapled pieces of yellowed graph paper on which my dad had hand-written detailed instructions (true to form for an engineer) about proper preparation for tennis matches. Although no date is attached, I'm certain he wrote it around the same time Coach Daub was training me. My dad's intent, I'm certain, was to help prepare me for competition at the professional level.

By this time, my dad had been around the sport for years and applied his considerable intellect, observational skills, and interest in my career choice into what I consider to be an impressive coaching document ahead of its time. It contains many of the core principles tennis pros teach aspiring players today. At the time, I neither took the time nor had the inclination to fully utilize it—yet another example of the dilemma parents face in advising their kids. Even when a parent has tremendous resources and insight, it's rare that a kid has the maturity to take full advantage. This was certainly true in my case. I'll highlight some of the key points in hopes that others might benefit more from my dad's advice than I did.

His thoughts were divided into four sections:

Overview

- Sleep properly but don't oversleep or nap between matches.

- No more than two beers within twenty-four hours of a match.

- If you've lost sleep, don't worry—adrenaline will compensate.

- Do isometrics and aerobics six days per week but no exercise (outside of normal tennis prep) the day of or before a match.

- Practice with intensity before each match using all shots. No "casual" shots and concentrate using the three key guidelines in match instructions (listed below).

Pre-Match Instructions

Play Point Tennis—using three key guidelines in match instructions (listed below). If you have a weak opponent, go for a twenty-four-point set. If you have a good opponent, make him win the last point (if you follow these instructions, he won't!).

- Accept that tennis, for you, is no longer "fun" or "pleasant"—it is all hard work. All you can get out of tennis is satisfaction in work and concentration.

- Don't lie to yourself—assume all opponents will be tough, either because they are or because you might play weak. You shouldn't be concerned an opponent might be stronger than you if you:

  - Accept that all opponents are going to try and win.

  - Accept that following these disciplines will allow you to beat most opponents.

  - Accept that nothing will demoralize you more than losing to an opponent you underestimated.

- Keep your feelings hidden—anger shows your opponent you believe he is stronger. Anger leaves you believing you can't play the next point better. Anger causes you to lose points because you lose the fans (you win more points when you know the fans are with you) and default after your second outburst in any match (it won't matter in the big picture and will improve your future).

Match Instructions

- Play POINT tennis by concentrating ONLY on the following three key guidelines:

- #1 EYE ON BALL TO CONTACT

- #2 RACKET BACK EARLY

- #3 DECIDE ON SHOT QUICKLY AND STICK WITH IT

- If you're winning or even in score, stick with your strategy. If you're losing, change your strategy.

- Trick #1—If you are mentally trapped into thinking you are going to lose the next point, go for a flamboyant shot (lob, drop, angle, hit opponent, etc.).

- Trick #2—On your opponent's serve, *expect* to win the point if you make a deep return that negates the server's advantage. Play to win every point in which the server loses his serve advantage—DON'T LET UP!

Analysis of Match Instructions

If you do the three key guidelines on every point, you won't have the mental time to let down after a first set win/loss, come to believe your opponent is going to win, focus on being tired, or get "psyched" out of points.

- Trick #1—The shot you pick must be unexpected. This will work because: you were "willing" a lost point anyway. Going for a flamboyant shot breaks your negative train of thought, and the odds of winning on a thought-out flamboyant shot are higher than a conventional shot on a point you expected to lose.

- Trick #2—How many players do you play who can truly maintain their serve advantage once you get the ball back deep? Paradoxically, most players, including pros, expect to lose their opponent's serve. "Holding serve" has become the convention because the receiver permits it 90 percent of the time.

This was all written by a guy who never played high-level competitive tennis or had any training as a tennis pro. Not too bad. The older I've gotten, the smarter my parents have become. I doubt I'm alone in that realization. I probably heeded Coach Daub's advice about tennis back then more than my dad's. But I was indeed fortunate to have people like my father who cared enough about me to speak wisdom into my life—even when I wasn't paying attention.

CHAPTER 7
PRO TENNIS DIARIES

The gap between college and professional sports is much wider than most people realize. A few reasons come to mind. First, everyone who plays professionally has attained a high level of physical, mental, and tactical skills. In college, the margins aren't as small—you can win some matches even if you have an off day. That never happens at the pro level. And second, the barrier to entry into pro sports is much higher than in college. Just getting into a pro event, let alone winning prize money, can be extremely challenging.

Maybe it's best to illustrate this last point with a brief overview of how things worked when I attempted to break into pro tennis. (This was in 1983-84, during the time Coach Daub was training me and before I had moved on to grad school at

Temple.) You earn a world ranking, entry into tournaments, and prize money based on your ability to attain Association of Tennis Professionals (ATP) points—they're the holy grail for any pro tennis player. The prevailing school of thought was that the more remote the location, the more likely it was that you could earn ATP points because fewer players would go. Unfortunately, this was, for the most part, a flawed assumption. No matter how far I traveled, ATP points were awfully hard to come by. The entry level of pro tennis back then was called "satellite circuits" (now called challengers). These were a series of four circuit tournaments played in consecutive weeks in various cities, with a fifth week master's event. Entry into the master's was reserved for players who qualified based on their performance during the first four weeks. For example, if you were playing the Texas satellite, you might first play in Waco, Corpus Christi, Houston, and Austin. Based on your results, you might earn enough circuit points to enter the master's tournament the fifth week in Dallas. If you were playing in Spain, it would be the same thing, except you couldn't speak the language nor pronounce the names of the cities. Only the top thirty-two players moved on to play in the master's event, and here's the catch: the only way to earn ATP points—regardless of how well you played in the first four weeks—was to get into the master's tournament.

For guys like me, just breaking in, you had to play in a qualifying tournament just to get into the main draw of a circuit event.

These qualifying tournaments awarded no prize money, but typically, at least sixty-four players competed, all fighting for eight slots into the main draw each week. The competition for those eight slots was intense. Some of the most hard-fought matches I've ever seen, or been a part of, happened in some remote city, on a back court, with no spectators, during the qualifying event for a circuit tournament. It was entirely possible to play for four weeks and not qualify for a main draw—in which case you made no money, and more importantly, you didn't stand a chance of making the master's tournament and earning ATP points, which was the whole point. If none of this makes sense to you, that's okay. Here's the bottom line: getting your foot in the door of pro tennis is . . . really, really hard—which explains why so few people even stand a chance of making a living playing the sport.

So why attempt to play professional sports if the odds of success are so low? I think the reason is precisely that achieving success *is* so hard. If it wasn't, the thrill wouldn't be so great. Something about the challenge draws you in, captivates your attention, and motivates you to keep going; it's hard to articulate. It's like watching those documentaries on TV about people who climb mountains. Climbing makes them feel alive in ways that nothing else can, but they have trouble explaining what drives them to take such risks. Trying to make a living playing pro tennis is like that, albeit without the risk of death. The feelings it elicits are so powerful that they make whatever hardships you endure to achieve them worth the cost.

Landing on Another Planet

The first circuit I played as a professional was in Norway. Even though I was twenty-two, it was the first trip I'd ever taken outside of the United States. Traveling alone, I got on a plane at JFK Airport, flew to Frankfurt, Germany, boarded an all-night train, and arrived in Oslo on a gray, rainy morning not sure what day it was. I felt as if I was on another planet. I knew no one, couldn't understand a word anyone said, and had no place to stay. I did, however, have a piece of paper with the address of a tennis club.

I walked outside the train station and handed the address to a taxi driver. In about a half hour, we pulled up in front of someone's house in a suburb of Oslo. Having given up on verbal communication, he motioned for me to get out of the car. I thought, surely, we were in the wrong place. Nevertheless, after two days of travel, there I was in Norway carrying a racket bag and pushing a suitcase down the street. I felt the eyes of the people in the neighborhood looking out their windows, curious about the confused-looking man aimlessly walking the streets. I had no idea what to do next and wondered if pro tennis might not have been the greatest career choice.

Then I heard the faint *thwack* of tennis balls somewhere behind one of the houses. To get closer, I knew I would have to cut through someone's backyard. I figured I'd take the chance, hoping I wouldn't get shot by some crazed Norwegian. Sure enough, I found a tennis club back there. My stress level dropped a notch, as it seemed I was in the right place. I heard someone speaking English in a strange accent and followed that sound until I came upon a bunch of guys practicing on one of the back courts. They were a team of Australians traveling Europe with their coach. I explained the basics of my situation to one of the guys. The next thing I knew, I was in their van heading to a youth hostel where they were staying. They set me up with a room, pointed me to a restaurant nearby, and I was off and running on the pro circuit. I have never, before or since, felt that lonely and disoriented (and I'm writing this forty years later). Now, when people seem impressed that I played pro tennis, imagining the glamorous lifestyle that implies, I always think of that day—and have a good laugh to myself.

Getting Started (-ish)

I played one of the Australians in my first match. I really struggled acclimating to the slow, slippery red clay courts since I was more comfortable with the quicker bounce and sure footing of the hard courts back home. My opponent was a big, left-handed redhead named Nick Arnold. I played okay, all things considered, but unfortunately, he won the match 6–4 in the third set.

After losing highly competitive, heartbreaking matches like that, one of two things happens. Either you storm off the court in a cloud of emotion with your opponent becoming a villain in the fictional story you are writing in your head, or you sit in stunned silence considering early retirement from the sport. For some reason I chose the latter, and, to my surprise, Nick stopped by before heading off to report our scores to the tournament officials. What struck me was how genuinely relaxed he was, as if the match had been just another day at the office. He said something classically Australian, "Well played, mate." I got the feeling Nick would have said that regardless of whether he'd won or lost. I wasn't used to playing guys that could handle victory and defeat with such a good-natured ease.

It was a full week until the next tournament in a city I couldn't begin to pronounce. I had no transportation, no practice partners, and no idea how to deal with the loneliness of being on my own in a foreign country. I hung around the courts the rest of the day, not knowing what else to do with myself. I watched qualifying matches and occasionally caught glimpses of players in the main draw, scheduled to start in a few days. These guys looked well-rested, experienced, and better than me at tennis. They tended to travel in pairs (much smarter than my solitary approach) and had free rackets, coaches, and pretty girlfriends. They carried themselves with the quiet confidence born of success.

As the day came to an end, Nick appeared and asked if I needed a lift back to the hotel. I said sure, trying to act as nonchalant as I could. We grabbed our bags and headed toward the big white van in which Nick's coach was waiting with the Australian team, and I squeezed into the last remaining seat.

Australia has no college system for tennis, so if you wanted to turn professional, you had to do it right after graduating high school. Some teenagers in that group already had multiple years of experience on the pro circuit. Even though I was in my early twenties and had played four years of Division 1 college tennis, I felt like a rookie compared to those guys. But, as anyone who has ever spent time with Australians knows, they are among the most free-spirited, fun-loving, and genuine people you will ever come across. I fit in quickly, Nick and I became good friends, and I traveled around in that van with the Aussies for the rest of the circuit. I doubt anyone even asked their coach if he minded.

Adversity (My Constant Companion)

As an adopted member of the team, I now had transportation, practice partners, camaraderie, and a support system. It felt like being back in college except that I didn't have to go to class. The following week, the night before the matches were to start, I was practicing at about 10:30 p.m. (a uniquely Norwegian experience due to the long daylight hours at that time of year). I pushed off my left foot, like I had done countless times in my tennis life, to chase down a ball hit to my right. As I did so, my foot got caught in a small, undetectable divot on the poorly maintained court. My left ankle turned over so quickly that I had no possibility of reacting. All I remember was hearing a sharp popping sound and then rolling around on the red clay.

I limped back to the dorms and propped my foot up on my bunk bed. By now it was around 11 p.m. My ankle was visibly swollen. I didn't feel like limping into the shower, so I just lay there with red clay stuck to my sweaty clothes.

Once again, an Australian appeared. This time it was a guy named James Fitzpatrick. He noticed my ankle and, with typical Australian good humor, said, "So, whatcha got there, mate?" I gave him the basic facts but wasn't much in the mood to elaborate. We had a brief discussion, which concluded with me proclaiming that I intended to tape it up and play the next day. I could tell James was not terribly optimistic. I didn't sleep much since my ankle was killing me, I still hadn't taken a shower, and I was more than a little despondent about my situation.

The next morning as I put my left foot on the floor, pain shot up through my leg—there was no way I could walk. As I sat staring at my ankle, now nearly twice its normal size, James appeared with the keys to the van and said, "Hey, mate, we're taking a ride." He said he was taking me to find a doctor to look at my ankle. I remember protesting, under the delusion that I needed to stick around in hopes of playing later that day. But another thing about Australians I was learning was that they can be tough characters. James was not asking me; he was telling me.

He helped me limp to the van, and we drove around in hopes of finding a medical facility—this was years before cells phones, Google, and GPS. We finally found a hospital and walked into the emergency room. Using sign language, we communicated the best we could. About two hours later, I had been X-rayed and examined by a doctor who could speak a little English. He explained that I had torn ligaments in my ankle and that the protocol in Norway was to repair it with surgery, which he offered to schedule within the next few days. James and I concluded it was best to think about this a bit. We thanked the doctor and left the hospital.

I called home and learned that the protocol in the States with an injury like mine was to rehab for four to six weeks rather than operate. I decided to stay in Norway for the remainder of the circuit and see if I could play the next one scheduled for Holland in about four weeks' time. I spent those weeks traveling with the Australians, getting rides from James into town for rehab, and watching a lot of tennis. So . . . what's the moral of this story? First, if you are going to play professional tennis, whether in the US or in a foreign country, never travel without a friend, practice partner, and someone who can help you out in emergencies. Second, Australian people are the best—this needs no elaboration. Third, sometimes being lucky is better than being smart. I was the embodiment of this concept on that trip to Norway. And finally, as I mentioned earlier, though being a professional tennis player may sound glamorous, the reality often is quite the opposite.

Breaking Through (Kind Of)

When I arrived in Holland four weeks later for the next circuit, my ankle was still shaky, but I was able to tape it up and play matches. The first few weeks were challenging. I didn't win many matches—certainly not enough to qualify for any of the main draws. The Australian guys weren't playing the circuit in Holland, but a few other Americans had showed up and I started to practice with them. Also, many of the tournaments provided housing for the players, so I had a chance to meet some wonderful Dutch families. I even got used to riding a bike everywhere since that's the prevailing form of transportation in Holland.

At the fourth and final tournament on the circuit I won two matches, which put me in the qualifying round for the main draw. Finally, I started to feel as if I belonged on the circuit, even though my match would be played in a remote town, on a back court, with zero spectators. I had played in preseason matches back in college with more people watching. However, fortunately for me, an umpire was assigned to the match. He sat in one of those high chairs next to the court, like a lifeguard making sure we didn't drown in the rip current of minor league pro tennis. I played an American named Andrew Gonzales, who had been playing for about five years at this level. He was ranked in the top 300 in the world, although he had never broken through to the big leagues of pro tennis.

As we took the court, Andrew seemed irritated that he had to play in the qualifying tournament—as if playing me was barely worth his time. Apparently, he had just missed the cutoff for the main draw. I doubt he figured he'd have much trouble beating me. I, on the other hand, looked at the match as if it were the finals of Wimbledon. I played well and found myself up a set and winning in the second. Right about this time, the weather changed, and it started to drizzle. Andrew, knowing he had to change the momentum of the match, immediately went to the umpire, and demanded we stop playing. But red clay courts are designed to absorb moisture, so the court conditions were just fine. Also, all the other matches were still in progress. Thankfully, the umpire ruled the match would continue.

With a renewed sense of urgency, I quickly closed out the match. Afterward, I sat in a small restaurant at the club savoring the win. Other players, many of whom I'd never met, started to stop by. Some were Americans, but most were guys I recognized from the circuit back in Norway who could barely speak English. Andrew had earned a reputation for being a bit of a prima donna, so the guys seemed glad he had lost. But mostly they congratulated me for overcoming the ankle injury I had sustained back in Norway. It was gratifying to feel as if I'd earned the respect of my peers—it meant more than anything a coach, parent, or girlfriend could have said at that moment.

However, in the world of pro tennis, you don't have long to celebrate wins. That's because guys like me who have just fought their way through three rounds of qualifying usually, if not always, play one of the highest seeded players in the first round of the main draw. None of those top seeds had to play three rounds of qualifying matches. The next morning, although I wasn't completely outclassed, I lost to one of the top players in the tournament. I had been in Europe for ten weeks and, due to injury, had played only five tournaments. I qualified for a main draw in the last event but never came close to earning an ATP point or getting a world ranking, which was the whole point of going over there. Welcome to the world of pro tennis.

The End of the Road

Over the next year, I played a circuit in Texas and a few local prize money tournaments. My next (and last) trip to Europe was to Yugoslavia and Spain. Having learned my lesson about traveling alone the previous year, I went with two guys I knew from college. The plan was to play three circuits: one in Yugoslavia, then two in Spain, all over a three-month span.

We flew to Vienna, Austria, rented a car, and drove over the Alps into Yugoslavia. When we got to the border, stern military men greeted us with machine guns. We realized quickly that living in Yugoslavia in 1984 was going to take some adjustment. It was an insanely beautiful country, but everything felt . . . dark. People rarely smiled, the roads were bad, the grocery stores were barely stocked, and the men working outside openly drank vodka at 10 a.m. I preferred the loneliness of Norway to the depression of Yugoslavia. Thankfully, having companions from the States with me helped. Our hope was that in such a far-flung location, the competition would not be as strong. That myth was quickly dispelled when we found that 128 guys showed up for the qualifying event the first week just to compete for eight spots in the main draw.

I don't think any of us qualified for any main draws during that circuit. We drove back to Vienna and boarded a plane for Spain. By this time, living out of a suitcase, traveling constantly, staying in cheap hotels, and eating lots of pizza was becoming second nature to me. I won some matches but rarely, if ever, made it to a main draw. If I did, I was promptly taken out by a seeded player in the first round.

After about six weeks and near the end of the second circuit in Spain, we were on the island of Mallorca, one of the most beautiful places I've ever visited. We were all having a blast, but I was getting depressed from losing so often. It was at this tournament that I had the biggest meltdown of my tennis career. During the warmup of my first match, after sizing up my opponent, I determined that I should have a good chance to win. But within just a few minutes, I found myself down 6–1, 5–0. At the changeover, I sat down and had a complete emotional breakdown, tearing up as I tried to cover my face. I decided I was going to quit tennis after losing the next game. I visualized packing my gear, getting in a taxi to the airport, flying home, and starting a new life.

But I won the next five straight games to get to 5–5. Since I had already decided I was quitting tennis and the outcome of the match didn't matter, I relaxed, trusted myself, and just played the game. At that moment, I remember thinking I might not quit after all. But as I started the next game, I could feel the old thought patterns creeping back. I started to think rather than do, try rather than trust. I quickly lost the next two games. After the match, I sat in my chair next to the court feeling despair unlike any I'd ever experienced. I had worked hard, improved a lot, beaten a few highly ranked players, and enjoyed some amazing life experiences, but a weak link remained in my psychological chain. As Dr. Loehr, my sports psychologist, pointed out when I returned, I had come to the game late from a mental skills standpoint. I'd made some progress, but it was too little, too late—and I wasn't making enough money to support myself as a pro tennis player. I was at the crossroad at which all athletes arrive sooner or later. I knew it was time to move on.

Living the "glamorous" life of pro tennis, somewhere in Spain.

CHAPTER 8
HITTING WITH TIM

Fortunately, even after my pro career ended, I continued to have the opportunity to share the court with world-class touring pros. Those interactions resulted in nuggets of wisdom that I applied to my own life and passed along to countless students throughout the years.

Just after I moved to Charlotte, North Carolina, in January 1987, I got a call from Tim Wilkison asking me to practice with him. Tim had been ranked among the top thirty players in the world, and the TV commentators had nicknamed him "Dr. Dirt" due to his hustle and intensity on the court. I assumed big-time pros like Tim spent the bulk of their time wandering the globe living in nice hotels, eating out for every meal, and practicing with their private coaches. But as it turned out, Tim lived in Charlotte and was a normal, down-to-earth guy. Still, I had mixed feelings about practicing with him. It was a great opportunity to hit with such an accomplished player, but I wondered if I'd be able to give him much practice. I kept my reservations to myself and agreed to meet him at a local club at 6:30 a.m. I'd rarely, if ever, practiced at that time. But apparently, this was standard for him—and so began a master class on what it takes to be a successful touring pro.

What I learned from Tim redefined how I thought about the sport. He didn't teach me anything I hadn't known before; he just executed on a much higher level. His example was more powerful than any words could have been. Starting his training day so early was just the beginning. When I arrived, Tim was already stretched out, warmed up, and ready to go. As we started, I was surprised that I could hit comfortably with him. But just as my nervousness started to fade, I realized that the guy just *never* missed, so I was expending every bit of mental and physical energy I had simply to keep rallies going—and we were only ten minutes into the workout. I wondered how I could keep it up, particularly if we played points and I had to cover the whole court.

As my mind wandered, I started to miss. This provided me with a welcome opportunity to catch my breath. The problem was that Tim didn't take breaks; he immediately fed another ball and came to the net to hit volleys. This meant the distance between us shrunk, and the tempo of the rallies increased. My heart rate went through the roof. Tim, on the other hand, hadn't broken a sweat. Thankfully, he suggested we hit a few serves and then play some points. For a few minutes, at least, I could recover. I did, however, have a feeling that things were about to get more challenging once we started to compete. I envisioned a few potential issues. Tim covered the court well, rarely made unforced errors, and didn't seem to get tired. That meant I would have to hit multiple great shots just to win one point. And as anyone who's ever played tennis knows, this is hard to do for any length of time.

Also, his intensity was intimidating. I could feel it from the other side of the court. Tim looked like he was playing a match I had watched him play on TV the previous year, which had been *in the quarterfinals at the US Open*.[11] It didn't seem to matter to him that our "match" was before breakfast on a back court with no spectators, prize money, or TV audience. I'd never seen anyone as disciplined about practice as Tim. I've often wondered how good I'd have been if I'd have approached things the same way before I met him.

Over the next few years, I practiced with Tim many times and got to know him fairly well. Occasionally when I returned from a practice session, I would write a few notes in order to solidify what I was learning. I've condensed them into two categories in the bullet points below. I think they contain lessons

---

11 https://www.washingtonpost.com/archive/sports/1986/09/02/wilkisons-rocky-act-is-a-triumph/f659afb3-c496-46eb-9dac-54cabbebcd1f/

for anyone wanting to succeed on the tennis court—or any sport, for that matter.

Notes to Myself

- *Make the most of every opportunity.* Show up early, even if practice is at 6:30 a.m. Try your hardest, even if you're overmatched. Not everyone gets a chance to practice with a player at Tim's level.

- *Turn on your joy.* Tim has been playing since he was a little kid and turned pro at seventeen. He still practices with childlike joy; his love for the game seems undiminished.

- *Prepare for everything.* Every day Tim works on hitting high backhand overheads. This was curious to me since that shot comes up so rarely in matches. I asked Tim why he did that, and he said he wanted to prepare for anything that may come up in a match, even if it's unlikely.

- *Maintain your standards.* Tim practices at full intensity even though he usually beats me easily—he looks no different playing me than he did playing in the quarterfinals of the US Open.

- *Make every point matter.* Once, after winning a routine point during a game to eleven, Tim reacted exuberantly with a big fist pump. This seemed over-the-top to me. When we finished, I asked him why he had made such a big deal of just one point. He explained that the score at the time was 7–4, and he wanted to increase his lead to 8–4. To me, this didn't seem like such a big deal, but when you played against Tim you always got the feeling that, to him, *every* point mattered.

- *Seek constant improvement.* One of Tim's best shots was his backhand, but I noticed he consistently worked on that shot anyway (through improving his ability to impart different spins on the ball). This was another way in which Tim was unique. He worked on improving his strengths, not just his weaknesses.

- *Cultivate gratitude.* Tim has been in the top 100 in the world for close to fifteen years. He mentioned recently that he still feels fortunate to be making a living playing tennis. I think that mentality is one big factor in his success. He takes nothing for granted.

- *Keep things simple.* Tim pays attention to technique, tactics, and emotional dynamics. But he doesn't overanalyze too much. He might sum up a poor match by saying, "I needed to move better," or evaluate an opponent by saying, "He gets frustrated easily." But he rarely lingers or gets bogged down in details.

- *Visualize the positive.* Once, while watching him play at a tournament, I asked Tim what the score was as he marched toward the baseline to serve. He quickly and with great resolve said, "One more game." To this day, it's the most unique answer I've ever gotten to that question. The match was over in just a few more minutes; I don't think I need to elaborate on the outcome.

Tim's Thoughts on Tennis

- *Coaching:* If you're a coach, it's a good idea to play tournaments. It keeps you fresh, involved in the game, and less hypocritical. You will relate better to students if you remember that it's easier to tell people what to do than to do it yourself.

- *Playing strong opponents:* Focus on being consistent, playing patterns of shots you're best at, and staying present-centered. Don't try and play "up" to their level; instead, trust in your own abilities. Make them beat you with great shots rather than beating yourself with too many errors. If they win, accept they were better than you that day. You didn't lose the match, they won it—there's a big difference.

- *Tactics:* Tactics in tennis are all about finding the balance between consistency and aggressiveness. And that will always be a challenge. It takes experience to know when and how to adjust your tactics during the changing dynamic of a tennis match (or in any competitive sport).

- *Momentum:* Tennis is a game of momentum shifts, so expect them to happen. Managing this is what competition is all about. The goal is to capitalize when you're up and limit the damage when you're down. When things are going poorly, don't panic. Stay focused and keep trying. When the momentum shifts back, ride it as long as you can.

- *Adversity:* Every match you play will present some form of adversity. If you don't accept that, you'll feel frustrated every time things don't go your way, which is a sure road to making things worse. Sometimes it just takes one good shot to turn things around. But you can't force that to happen; be patient and let it come to you.

- *Playing the score:* When up in a game, say 40–15 or 30–0, it's a good time to be aggressive. If you can hit a big forehand, go to the net, attack a weak second serve, and so on—go for it. There's an increased chance of missing, but the payoff is high. And since you already have the lead, there's less risk of losing the game.

- *Playing with a lead:* Think of playing with a lead like you are in a 100-yard dash and you've just pulled slightly ahead. Keep pushing for the finish line and resist the urge to look back. When we're winning, we tend to protect rather than project. We're often reactive rather than proactive. Better to keep playing the way you did to get the lead in the first place.

- *Look for "hidden points":* Learn to identify points that can result in big advantages. Good examples would be the first point of each game (which gives you the chance to build momentum early) or when the score is 30–15 (if you win that point, you can win the game on either of the next two points). Many players don't pay attention to those "hidden points," so make sure you do.

- *Don't pre-judge outcomes:* How your game style compares to your opponent's is more important than rankings or seedings. For example, a lower-ranked consistent player often has a good chance of beating a higher-ranked aggressive player, particularly if the latter has an off day. Game style matchups and mental toughness matter more than statistics or reputation.

- *Levels of the game:* Tim mentioned one day that what separated him from his competitors, even though they may look similar, was a 5 percent difference in ability level. The margins are small, which means that upsets are always possible. Over time, however, the better player will win more consistently. That's why it's important to keep any one bad loss or big win in perspective—the result of one match doesn't mean much in the big picture.

- *Intrinsic motivation:* Coaches can be of great value, but if you want to win badly enough, you'll do most of what coaches tell you to do anyway. In other words, if you truly wanted to succeed, you would compete for every point, run for every ball, and practice with intensity *without a coach having to tell you.* If your internal drive is strong, most of the details take care of themselves.

CHAPTER 9
ANATOMY OF A TENNIS TOURNAMENT

B y August 2001, at age forty, I was well into my life as a husband, father, and director of a tennis academy in Charlotte. I hadn't played competitive tennis for years. Nevertheless, for some reason, I decided to play in a tennis tournament. The tournament was the State 30 and Over Championship being played in High Point, North Carolina, about two hours from my house. When I returned from the tournament, I wrote a diary about the events of that long, painful weekend. The lessons I learned were not only helpful to my students in the coming years but applied to my life off the court as well.

Day 1 (Thursday)

Drove to High Point by myself, my head full of worldly concerns and already missing my family. Played a weaker player but barely won in two poorly played sets. I often forgot the score and struggled controlling the self-defeating, critical thoughts swirling through my head. Ate at a bad restaurant, stayed in a Motel 6, woke up at 2 a.m., and never fell back asleep. It seemed like a good idea to play this tournament, but now I'm not so sure. I found a Bible in the room, and as I read through some passages, had the distinct impression that God was teaching me to trust Him rather than my own abilities. I'm not sure where this came from, although this is something I've been struggling with back in the real world. Maybe this weekend, somehow, is His way of getting me to learn how to do this better. We'll see . . . probably a good idea to pay attention.

Day 2 (Friday Morning)

Played a decent player but someone I would usually beat about 6–3, 6–3. I played horribly and lost the first set 6–2. But something told me (let's call this an internal voice) to do my best, stay present centered, and JUST KEEP PLAYING. That last thought kept coming back into my head, small but insistent . . . JUST KEEP PLAYING. I didn't play much better but won the next two sets 6–4, 6–4—don't ask me how. We had started the match at 9 a.m. and as the morning wore on, it got hot and humid (no surprise for August in North Carolina). We finished at 11:30 and I was soaked with sweat. During the match I glanced at the court next door. I noticed that one of the players looked quite strong and won easily in about an hour. As I reported to the scorer's table, I found out that he would be my next opponent at 1 p.m. As my mind raced, I showered quickly, drove to a nearby Wendy's, ate part of a baked potato and a salad, stopped at a market to buy three Gatorades, and returned to the tournament site just in time for my match.

Day 2 (Friday Afternoon)

By this time, the sun was really beating down. I was playing poorly, still distracted, and starting to wear out physically. I resolved to do my best not to let my opponent see weakness. After particularly bad points in which I had made easy errors, I kept hearing that voice in my head . . . JUST KEEP PLAYING. So that's what I did. I won the first set 6–2 and felt that if I could play reasonably well *some of the time*, I'd have a good chance to win. I had remembered from my college days that players often look better from the sidelines than when you get on the other side of the net. This was no different; I knew I could beat this guy. Another holdover from college that worked in my favor was that I hated losing. Or to put it positively, I have a strong desire to win—I suppose they are two sides of the same coin.

I could tell my opponent thought that my winning the first set was an aberration, since he was a high seed in the tournament, younger by ten years, and had likely never heard of me. He started playing well, hustling for every ball, and looking as if he expected to win the match. The points were getting long, and we started to play some great points as the mid-afternoon sun beat down on us. We got to 2–2 on my serve and played one of the longest games of my life. Each of us had multiple game points but neither could close it out. Somewhere during the game my "hate to lose/will to win" DNA kicked in. I decided that no matter how tired I was getting, I was going to win that game. My mantra, JUST KEEP PLAYING, rattled around in my head. After a few more deuces and ads, I finally won it. And as we walked to our chairs at the change of sides, I could see it in his eyes—he was done. The spark he had shown earlier was gone; I could tell he didn't think he could beat me. I felt physically and mentally drained, but he didn't know that. I acted as if I could play all day and won the next four games in just a few minutes. The score was 6–2, 6–2, but I'll always remember that match as one of the toughest I'd ever played, mainly due to that interminable game at 2–2.

I reported my scores, threw my stuff in the car, and headed for home. There was no way I was going to stay in that Motel 6 again; I wanted to see my wife and kids, eat some good food, and sleep in my own bed. I took a few minutes to stretch before getting in the car in hopes of not cramping up on the drive.

As I did, a line from Vince Lombardi came to mind (I had recently read his biography): "I firmly believe that any man's finest hour—his greatest fulfillment to all he holds dear—is that moment when he has worked his heart out in a good cause and lies exhausted on the field of battle—victorious!" I know this might sound a bit melodramatic. I was just playing a silly thirty and over tennis tournament in High Point. But for me, at that moment, that quote resonated. I had just played seven sets of tennis in less than twenty-four hours, pushed myself to my limit, and was still in the tournament. It was a moment of self-satisfaction that's stayed with me ever since.

When I got home, I reflected on how self-centered you must be to succeed in tennis, which I'd never realized in my younger days. I stretched, took a bath with Epsom salts, ate dinner, and strung a racket as fast as I could. I barely acknowledged my wife and kids before heading straight for bed.

Day 3 (Saturday)

Got up early for the drive to High Point starting at 7:30 a.m. I did my best to stretch the soreness out of my legs, hit a few balls against a backboard, and took the court again in the semifinals against the number one seed. It was another hot and humid day. I still felt as if I was playing poorly; that feeling never seemed to go away. But I'd gotten in the habit of ignoring that voice and listening to the one that said JUST KEEP PLAYING. I noticed a trend that had been evident in all my matches. Whenever I got up in a game, I kept letting my opponent off the hook. I would consistently get up 30–0, 40–15, or even 40–0 and find myself playing deuce games that took forever. Sometimes I'd win the game anyway, but it was sapping energy from my already tired body. I continued to hide that fact from my opponent. I did, however, notice something positive—my opponent looked more tired than I was. After two hours on the court, I found myself up 6–4, 5–4, serving for the match. True to form, I went up in the game, let him back in it, and lost after some mindless unforced errors. We went to a tiebreaker at 6–6 in which I went up *again* for a 6–3 lead and three match points. I lost them all. Somehow, I barely won the tiebreaker 12–10. All I remember was telling myself to JUST KEEP PLAYING. By that time, I realized that was the only thing I could control.

Fortunately, the finals were scheduled for the next day, so I repeated the same routine as the night before. I drove home to briefly say hello to my family and prepare for the next day. It seemed like a lot had happened since Thursday night at the Motel 6. I was so absorbed in what I was doing that it felt as if a week had passed. I reminded myself that maybe God had some lessons for me in this whole experience. Maybe JUST KEEP PLAYING was His way of telling me to trust Him and ignore that critical self-dialogue born of the desire to rely on my own abilities. Of course, in matters like this, we never really know.

I did know that the same internal dynamics evident in that tournament were at work in my life off the court.

Day 4 (Sunday)

By this time, the road to High Point was quite familiar. When I arrived, a crowd was starting to congregate next to the court we would play on—this being a state championship match that would have some interest for the local tennis enthusiasts. I warmed up as best I could and took the court trying to look relaxed, confident, and ready to play. I knew my opponent would be a good player; otherwise, he wouldn't be in the finals, but I knew that regardless of what happened I would JUST KEEP PLAYING. I also reminded myself that no matter how tired, distracted, or self-critical I got, I'd do my best not to show that to my opponent. When the other guy only sees strength, resolve, and confidence on the other side of the net, especially if they are starting to lose theirs, it tends to be disheartening. As usual, I felt like I was playing poorly and lost the first four games quickly. However, I did realize something that I hadn't noticed up to that point. If I executed well, I won most of the points. In other words, if it was my best against theirs, my chances of winning were high. Something about this realization gave me confidence, even though I knew that consistently playing my best was a poor assumption given my track record thus far.

So . . . I just kept playing and won the first set before promptly going down 1–3 in the second. I came back to force a tiebreaker in which I found myself up 6–4 with two match points. True to form, I lost both points. But by that time, I was used to blowing leads. I told myself, one more time, to JUST KEEP PLAYING. Finally, during a long point with me up 8–7, I hit a short ball. My opponent attacked and came to the net. I got to the ball at the last second, off balance and out of position. But my training from previous years kicked in:

- Make your opponent hit one more ball rather than attempt an amazing shot.

- If you can touch the ball, *get it in.*

- Hit a shot you can make, even if it's likely your opponent will win anyway.

I reached out and pushed the ball crosscourt, accepting my fate. But in pressure moments, strange things sometimes happen. For some reason, he guessed I would hit the ball down the line and had overcommitted to that side. And since he was at the net, he didn't have enough time to recover. The ball went past him, and the tournament was over. I started walking to the net to shake his hand, and it took a moment to realize I'd won. I'd been so immersed in the match I hadn't thought about that possibility. As we shook hands, my opponent said something that I found so funny I had trouble keeping a straight face. He said that since I was in better shape than him, he doubted he could have won the third set even if he had won the tiebreaker. I said, "good match" and tried to conceal a smile. I doubted I'd ever play the guy again, but I figured it couldn't hurt if he thought I was Superman.

Takeaways

Time has rendered the outcomes of those matches meaningless to anyone but me. But the lessons I learned at that tournament were timeless. And they apply, I think, not just to competitive success on a tennis court, but to our lives outside of sports.

Challenge your assumptions.

When I first watched my opponents play, my initial thought was that they would be hard, if not impossible, to beat. But without exception, when I got on the other side of the court, I realized my chances were much better than I had thought. My tendency was, and is, to overestimate my opponents' abilities relative to my own. The difference between our thoughts (based on our limited, flawed, and biased perceptions) and reality is often much wider than we realize. As Coach Daub used to tell me, act on the objective not the subjective. In other words, when it comes to sports (or life), don't pre-judge outcomes. Let the results take care of themselves and never assume anything . . . just keep playing.

Stay in the present.

The one thing I consistently did well at that tournament was that I just kept playing, regardless of the circumstances. That mantra encapsulated everything I had ever learned about sports psychology. The ability to move on from the past, good or bad, and fully engage in the next point saved me from certain mental implosion. While I wanted to win the tournament, the thought of winning rarely entered my mind until after the last point was played. On the court, no past or future existed, just me hitting the next shot—at least most of the time.

Keep your feelings to yourself.

Many times my body was tired, and my mind raced with distracting, self-critical thoughts. But I had learned years before not to show weakness or let my opponents see me flustered. As a result, I think my opponents believed I was stronger than they were. I doubt that was true, but what mattered was their perception, not the reality. That gave me a subtle, but powerful, competitive advantage.

"You are not your thoughts."

I recently came across a book with that title. The basic premise was that we all have minds that constantly produce thoughts; some are productive, others not so much. But we can choose which of those thoughts we allow ourselves to dwell on.

I had lots of wild, anxious, self-defeating thoughts during that weekend. But I learned to disregard most of them and move on to the next point. You can't stop a thought from coming into your head but, most of the time, our thoughts don't accurately reflect reality. It's best to choose the ones we pay attention to.

There's no substitute for preparation.

I had subconsciously assumed, that I'd have a good chance to win this tournament based on previous experience in similar events. But sports (and life) are like the stock market—past results do not guarantee future performance. I still had remnants of the physical skills I possessed in my earlier days, my fitness level enabled me to survive the ordeal (barely), and I had some mental capacity. However, the big hole in my preparation was that I hadn't played full sets of tennis in a few years. In tennis terminology, we call this not being match tough. And the only way you can be match tough in tennis is to play tennis matches. I had no right to expect success without having taken the time and effort to prepare well. I was truly fortunate that things worked out that weekend for me.

Willpower can make all the difference.

Clearly, I still had a strong will to win, or hatred of losing—depending on how you look at it. This came into play many times during the tournament, particularly at 2–2 in the second set on Friday afternoon. I set my mind to doing everything I could to win that game, and once I did, the outcome of the match was a foregone conclusion. I'm not sure where this quality comes from, but it certainly is useful. Although, I must say the power of will is a poor substitute for good preparation.

It's more meaningful when it's hard.

I realized at the end of the second day that the tournament had become much harder than I had anticipated (a great example of how thoughts don't reflect reality). That's when Vince Lombardi's quote came to mind, "I firmly believe that any man's finest hour—his greatest fulfillment to all he holds dear—is that moment when he had worked his heart out in a good cause and lies exhausted on the field of battle—victorious!" While that may be true, I don't think winning the tournament mattered much in the big picture. The real value was in what I learned from the experience that I could apply in life. Being pushed to my limits provided that opportunity.

Pay attention to the details.

Success during that tournament required me to take care of every detail off the court—hydration, sleep, stretching, warmup, equipment, pain management, food intake, and so on. I had forgotten how self-obsessed you must be to win tennis matches. This is one of the reasons I decided to stop playing tournaments after this event. Winning tennis tournaments was no longer a high priority in my life. However, attention to detail was something that applied in every other area. I know that success is never guaranteed in any arena. Just like in a tennis match, there are too many variables that I can't control. However, taking care of the details is one thing I *can* do to improve my chances.

Listen to that other voice.

The first night of that tournament, as I lay awake in the Motel 6, it occurred to me that God might have something to teach me that weekend. I learned many lessons: the power of living in the present, how to choose the objective vs. the subjective (meaning not trusting my own thoughts), the importance of focusing on process rather than outcome, and the benefits (and limitations) of personal willpower. I think all these principles apply to spiritual life as well as athletic pursuit. I believe the lessons I learned were meant to teach me more about the former than the latter. From an early age, I had internalized the idea that hard work is what leads to success. And to a certain point, I still believe that's true. Sometimes, however, it's better simply to do your best and leave the results to a higher power (if you are so inclined spiritually, this can be a life-altering realization). I think this tournament helped me understand this concept at a deeper level. The voice that told me to "just keep playing" was, I think, God's way of teaching me to rely less on my own limited abilities, stay focused on what was right in front of me—and trust Him with the results down the road.

I had won five tennis matches in two-and-a-half days, against good players ten years younger, in the middle of the Carolina summer, with limited practice and a forty-year-old body. That tournament was the culmination of all the skills I'd accumulated over twenty-five years playing competitive tennis. This was a good feeling. But the sense of satisfaction wasn't high enough to justify continuing. Even if I could win a tournament like that again, which was doubtful, it wouldn't be worth the time and energy. And applying the lessons I learned to other areas of my life would provide more than enough challenge. It was finally time to retire from tournament tennis—and that was just fine with me.

CHAPTER 10
POWERFUL
RELATIONSHIPS

O ne of my favorite quotes about sports goes like this, "An athlete leaves only statistics and memories."[12] And while that's true to some degree, I think there's still great value in the pursuit of athletic excellence. The wins and losses become less important as time passes, and some of the memories may fade. However, the life skills you learn, the character you develop, and, most importantly, the relationships you build have lifelong impact.

For example, the relationships I formed in college were some of the most meaningful and longest-lasting I've ever

---

12 Al Laney quoted by Frank Deford in *Over Time*, p. 139

had. When you play on a sports team in college, you live, eat, sleep, and breathe with your teammates—like it or not—so the bonds I formed with them became quite strong. Living together so closely creates the potential to become each other's worst enemies or best friends. Thankfully, the latter applied in my case. I think the dynamics are somewhat analogous to being in the military, just without the shooting.

Team picture, junior year

People came and went during my years at Penn State due to a variety of issues (injury, school challenges, philosophical differences with Coach, character issues, and so on). There were only two guys with whom I played all four years. Everyone on the team had nicknames, so Jon Whiteside was "Whitey," Tom Beckhard was "Beeks," and I was "Schill." To this day, I know I can call them anytime and we'll pick up right where we left off. But I still have trouble calling them by their given names.

Don Ho

One guy in particular impacted me in a unique way, even though he was only at Penn State for two years. His name was Don Lowry and he was from Santa Barbara, California. We nicknamed him "Don Ho" after a Hawaiian singer who was popular in the '60s—I have no idea how we came up with this.

Don Ho became a legendary figure with the guys on our team. He had played number one for Santa Barbara Junior College before, somehow, Coach recruited him to come all the way out to Penn State and play for us. He arrived on campus my sophomore year in a beat-up Mazda pickup truck that he had just driven cross-country. When we saw him play tennis, we immediately knew he would be one of our best players. But what most impressed us was what a cool dude Don Ho was—his friendly personality, good looks, and laid-back California vibe appealed to everyone. Not to mention, walking everywhere at Penn State gets tiring and his truck came in handy.

I was living in a two-bedroom house just off campus with a few other guys (known to our friends on campus as "The Tennis House"). We invited him to live with us, so Don Ho and I became roommates and best friends. We shared a love for tennis, of course, but had many other common interests. He expanded my horizons in many areas (some of which may not have been legal at that time) and told me that I was a Californian at heart. One of our shared interests was music. Even now, much of the music I listen to is influenced by Don Ho.

I still have the audio cassette tapes he compiled for me during those years. Since my Sony Walkman is long gone, I now listen regularly to a Spotify playlist I put together inspired by those tapes (whenever I listen to Loggins and Messina, Joe Walsh, or The Doobie Brothers, I always think of Don Ho).

The only time any conflict came up between us was when we had to play a challenge match to determine who would play number one for the team. Challenge matches always had the potential to stir up trouble. I don't remember any details of this specific match except that it was highly competitive, and I barely came out on top. But something left a bad taste in Don Ho's mouth, likely due to some arrogant or obnoxious behavior on my part. This was, at that time, part of my DNA and not something I was consciously aware of. It must have lingered because the next day we ended up getting into a brawl back at the house, with our roommates having to pull us apart. But boys will be boys, as they say, and by the next day we had moved on. It felt no different to me than fighting with my brother.

As we got to know Don Ho better, my teammates and I noticed that Don Ho was kind of a free spirit. He would disappear regularly to go trout fishing in the mountains that surrounded Penn State. It seemed he preferred the serenity of a mountain stream to the rigors of the classroom. One day as the team was starting practice, we noticed Don Ho was missing. I surmised he had just gone fishing and lost track of time, until one of the guys showed up and mentioned a rumor going around that Don Ho had been spotted that afternoon driving a motorcycle up the steps of Pattee Library, Penn State's main library in the center of campus. If that were true, I figured it might be best for him to lay low in case the campus police were looking for the culprit. Pattee did have some nice steps that might be fun to ascend on a motorcycle. But, as far as I knew, no one had ever chosen that as an extracurricular activity.

I did know, however, that Don Ho was a "think out of the box" kind of guy. I asked him about the rumor when I got back to the house. Don Ho was cryptic and didn't share any details. However, the circumstantial evidence was compelling: one of the guys on the team had recently asked if he could store his motorcycle at our house for the winter. Don Ho had suggested that we "rent" him the space in exchange for being able to ride the bike—so there was that. I should have checked to see if the engine was warm.

Anyway, in my eyes, Don Ho's mystique continued to grow. One day I was visiting some friends in the dorms, and as I came out of the elevator to head home, I heard some beautiful music coming from a piano in the lobby. Curious, I headed toward the sound to find Don Ho deeply immersed in playing an improvised jazzy composition. I stood behind him for a while enjoying the music, waiting for him to finish. I asked where he had learned to play like that. He said nowhere; he was self-taught and just messing around. I had no idea that someone with no training could become that accomplished . . . clearly, there was more to this guy than met the eye.

As Don Ho's second year with us started, I noticed he was spending less time in school and more time fishing. He brought back some beautiful trout that lived in our freezer—although I can't recall ever eating any of them. Sometime that year, during a party at our house, Don Ho thought it might be interesting to leave one of the frozen trout in the toilet with the lid closed, the fish positioned with eyes facing up for

Don "Ho" Lowry, back in Santa Barbara, where the fish are bigger and the sun's always shining.

maximal effect. We would stand at a discreet distance, watch the bathroom door close, and wait for people's reaction. This form of entertainment, made possible through the creative imagination of Don Ho, provided yet another great memory from his time with us. But we all knew it couldn't last. It was clear that Don Ho belonged in California. I still remember the bittersweet feeling as I watched his truck pull out of the driveway at the end of the year, loaded up and bound for Santa Barbara. He had become one of my best friends, but I knew he wouldn't be coming back. However, his legend lives on in the minds and hearts of the guys who were lucky enough to share those years with him.

Coach

When my college teammates and I reminisce, many of our favorite stories revolve around our Penn State coach, Holmes Cathrall. We spent every day of the week under his charge at practice. Most weekends, we were roving around in a smelly Ford Econoline van like a pack of tennis-racket-wielding gypsies. Coach not only handled all the recruiting, coaching, logistics, and administration, he also dealt with team dynamics, girlfriend issues, loud music, and whatever mayhem came up overseeing people on the cusp of adulthood. We were old enough to be trusted with the basics but immature enough to require constant oversight. There had to have been times when Coach wanted to relax and let his guard down; of course, those were the moments when things would most likely go wrong.

One time on our yearly Southern Trip to Chapel Hill, North Carolina, we could find no place to sleep other than the floor of a fraternity house. We had two rooms and drew straws to determine which guys had to sleep in the same room with Coach, who was renowned for being the world's loudest snorer. One of the guys who drew a short straw along with me was Don Ho. He was the team DJ and the keeper of the boom box, which was equipped with a tape deck. At some point during the night, Don Ho had enough. It was literally impossible to sleep in the same room with Coach. So, in a moment of divine inspiration, he decided to record Coach's snoring. He put in a blank tape, pressed record, crawled over, and put the boombox six inches from Coach's face. I thought this would make for a fun moment the next morning when we played it back for him. But that was not what Don Ho had in mind.

He rewound the tape, cranked up the volume, put the speaker next to Coach's head, and pressed play. Within a few seconds, Coach jolted awake to the sound of his own snoring and a roomful of college kids laughing themselves silly. Somehow, Coach took it all in stride. He was back to sleep and was snoring again minutes later. As I lay awake, I couldn't help but wonder if he was dreaming that he had chosen a different profession.

Fortunately for us, Don Ho's prank in Chapel Hill ended benignly. But we all knew that we took our chances if we went too far. That is exactly what happened later during that trip. We had all walked downtown—the name of the school and location are now lost in my memory—to have a few beers. Upon returning, we found the room dark and Coach sound asleep. We weren't in the mood to sleep and, on top of that, some of the guys were hungry. We thought it might be a good idea to get some food at Denny's, since we knew it would be open at that late hour. But Denny's was a few miles away. The only way to get there would be to take the van. We were not, *technically*, allowed to drive the van, so we would need to wake Coach, or borrow the van and return it without Coach knowing. After some deliberation, and in a moment of epic stupidity, we chose the second option.

The key was in the pocket of Coach's jacket, which was hanging on his bedpost. We picked Whitey as the ninja to perform this delicate procedure. He was the most responsible, mature guy on the team, plus he drank the least, so he was the likeliest candidate to drive the van (although we hadn't gotten that far in our planning yet). Whitey snuck up next to Coach in the darkened room as we looked on. After a seemingly interminable silence, he pulled his hand from Coach's pocket and held up a set of dentures! The whole room burst out in laughter. Coach woke up from a deep sleep and within seconds assessed what was going on. I'd never seen him that angry.

With a few choice words that I won't repeat here, he directed the whole team to get our asses in the van. The room went completely silent. We bolted for the van and sat quietly in the dark, nervously awaiting what would happen next. A few minutes later, Coach appeared, got in the driver's seat, slammed the door, and floored it towards Denny's as we bounced around in the back of the van. He mumbled a few words about "taking us to the woodshed," which didn't sound too appealing when dealing with an ex-Marine. Not another word was spoken until he skidded to a stop in front of the restaurant. We all piled out of the van; Coach stayed right where he was in the driver's seat, which confused us since we knew he *loved* Denny's. This was uncharted territory for all. We ate quickly, sheepishly got back in the van, and retired for the night back at the dormitory.

The next morning, to our amazement, Coach delivered no lecture or punishment. For this, I am eternally grateful. I think he knew that we feared that woodshed, wherever that might be. Coach, if you are listening from up in heaven, I would like to say on behalf of the guys, *We're sorry! We love you, and thanks for putting up with us.*

The Freshmen

By my senior year, the guys on the tennis team had become like family to me—no doubt due to the many experiences we shared in the preceding years. But that fall, a freshman on our team named Virgil Christian had a surprising and monumental impact on my life. One night, Virgil called the house before one of our parties to ask if he could bring some girls he had met from the dorms. This was an obvious yes, although I reminded myself that Virgil was, after all, just a freshman. During my shift as a greeter later that evening, Virgil appeared. Behind him, some attractive young women were lined up single-file on the sidewalk. As Virgil introduced each one, his status in my eyes grew.

As the group trickled past, I noticed an impressive young lady named Liz. Penn State had plenty of pretty girls, but something was different about this freshman. To this day, I can't quite put my finger on it; let's just say she had a combination of personality and presence that I found . . . particularly attractive. I followed her down to the basement and the keg of beer, the first stop for any newcomer to our parties. I struck up a conversation, and the rest, as they say, is history. As I write this, we've been married for almost thirty-eight years. I'll leave the details for another book (maybe).

Me and Virgil, senior year

For the rest of the year, I did get some pushback from Whitey and Beeks for dating a freshman. Fortunately, I stuck to my guns. I made my share of poor decisions in college, but dating Liz wasn't one of them. I never miss an opportunity to thank Virgil for inviting her that night.

***

Quite often when athletes retire, they talk about how much they'll miss playing their sport. What I think they'll miss just as much are the relationships their sport made possible. As much as I loved to succeed on the court, those moments weren't meant to last forever, just enjoyed as they occurred. But tennis provided an environment through which many of the most important relationships in my life evolved—personal connections that impacted me far beyond the time I spent with a racket in my hand. And the people that mattered most were those who cared more about me as a person than for my accomplishments in the tennis world. When I think about all the people I met, either directly or indirectly, through tennis, I can unreservedly say that those relationships mean more to me than any success I achieved *playing the game.*

About the Author

After graduating from Penn State University where he was captain and played #1 in singles and doubles, Bill Schillings competed on the professional tennis tour both in the United States and abroad. He then served as an assistant tennis coach at Temple University, where he received his MA in sports administration.

Bill is a USTA High Performance Coach, USPTA Elite Professional, and was recognized as the NCTA 2016 Tennis Professional of the Year. He owned and directed Charlotte Tennis Academy from 1989-2022 where he coached and mentored countless juniors.

Bill published his first book, *Sports Parenting; Creating an environment for success . . . without going Bat Sh*t Crazy*, in 2022. He continues to coach part-time, writes about his experiences in tennis, and plays pickleball whenever possible. He also enjoys spending time with his family, which now includes two cute grandkids. Bill and his wife, Liz, live in Charlotte, North Carolina.